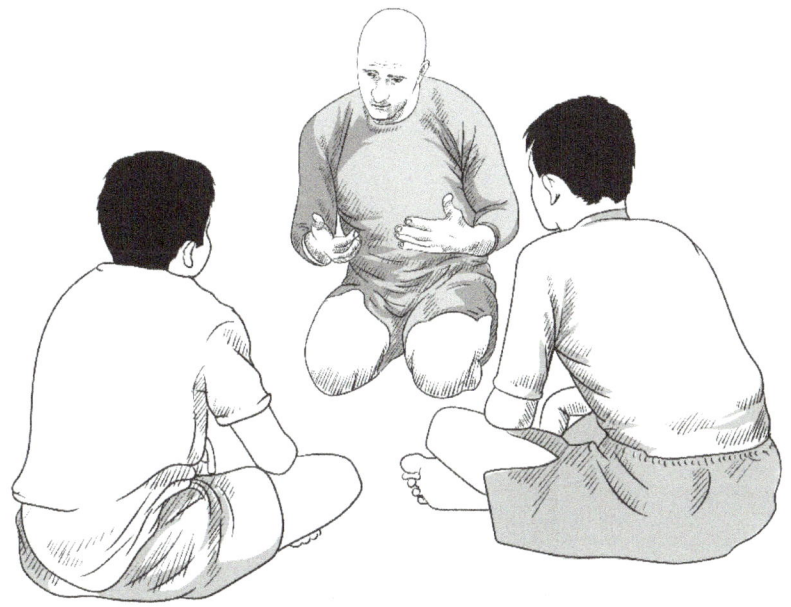

The Danaher Diaries

2021 Edition

Compiled by Heroes of the Art

FORWARD

The success of the Danaher Diaries "anthology" has been nothing short of amazing. We were tempted to leave the work complete with the release of the third volume in 2020. But Danaher had more to say and so did we. In addition to the technical and philosophical musings we have come to expect from John Danaher's social media, 2021 proved eventful in other ways. John left his longtime home base in New York to establish his own school in Puerto Rico. He took his team with him, and it seemed as if the "Danaher Death Squad" was truly beginning a new chapter.

Despite high hopes that his new location and team would continue their legendary run in the competitive circuit, the experiment was short lived. The greatest grouping of jiu-jitsu talent in a generation was unable to get established in their new environment, and several months into their adventure Danaher announced on social media that "the squad" would be splitting into two distinct groups. Both would be leaving Puerto Rico to return to the continental United States. Specifically, Texas. While many names in John's team were to disassociate themselves, two key names would remain: Gordon Ryan and Garry Tonon.

A second loss would be added to Danaher's year when Gordon Ryan announced a long-term hiatus from competing due to health issues. His announcement was carefully worded and many speculated that the world had not seen the last of him. For the first time in a decade, Danaher did not have the majority of the top ten grapplers in the world under his tutelage. Some may argue he never did, and others would point out that John still had many excellent students under him that had simply not become household names yet.

2021 Edition

Regardless, as Danaher relocated to Texas in the summer of 2021, his stock in the grappling world had a definite question mark next to it. Could he pick up where he left off and rebuild his notorious "Danaher Death Squad" to its former infamy?

Because this "book" is real life and not a story, the answer has yet to be written. But even if the resolution isn't clear, 2021 seemed to play out more like a story for John than any other year. That's why we decided to write the *entire* year and title it the 2021 edition. Sprinkled into Danaher's technical breakdowns of jiu-jitsu are his occasional updates about his personal life and the comings and goings of his team.

It's our hope that it all makes for fascinating reading, tracing a sort of oral history of a year in the life of John Danaher. An exceptional year. In this edition, we've also worked to make the book more aesthetically satisfying. We've heard the feedback on volumes one through three and we've worked to tighten up the formatting and even hire an artist for some original works sprinkled throughout the text. If you're reading this in our new hardcover version, we hope it "pops" on your coffee table, or the counter to your academy. If you are listening to this as an audiobook, we hope that the soothing cadence of our narrator helps you settle in for that car ride home after jiu-jitsu, where you can replay the events of the night in your head.

So, enjoy this year's edition of the Danaher Diaries, our largest and most polished yet. Like jiu-jitsu itself, it can never reach perfection. But *kaizen* demands that we try.

See you in the new year.

HAPPY NEW YEAR FROM THE SQUAD!!

Wishing you all the best for 2021!! Thank you all for your interest in the incredible work of my students and our philosophy of Jiu jitsu. We hope to show much more of our work around the Jiu jitsu world in the coming year - hopefully fate proves kinder to Jiu Jitsu this year than last, but whatever happens, dedication and determination will always prevail over hard times - wishing you all a great night and an even better year!

Why stay in front of opponents when you can get behind them:

To a large degree Jiu jitsu is the skill of maneuvering behind opponents. Sure, you can finish people from frontal positions, but nothing will match the relative ease and certainty of getting behind people and working from there. Try to make this PROGRESSION TO THE BACK an IMMEDIATE REFLEX in your part. Opportunities don't last long in competitive matches so the earlier you make your move the better in most cases. Just as you wouldn't accept being in front of an opponent's legs when playing against an opponent's guard, but rather always seeking to get around his legs to the side, so to from turtle position always seek to get past your opponent's arms and get to the back. Of course, there will be times when you may favor frontal attacks such as Guillotines or other strangles from the front, but your default option should always be to go behind your opponent.

Defensive soundness before submission:

The great cliché of Jiu jitsu is "position before submission" However, in some situations such as Ashi Garami, conventional approaches to position don't really apply, since both athletes are in a situation where they can attack each other at the same time. I'm these types of scenarios "position before submission "gets replaced by "defensive soundness before submission." The idea is to set your feet, knees and other relevant body parts in locations where they are defensively sound (not open to obvious attacks) prior to launching your own attacks. In this way you avoid the undesirable situation of both athletes attacking simultaneously, in which case victory will go to the faster athlete or the one who is prepared to lose a limb to break his opponent's limb. The best way is always that of first making yourself defensively sound so that when you do attack you can do so without the distraction of simultaneous counter attacks. Don't get into submission shoot outs if you can avoid them. Rather, create situations where you can fire at will without return fire. Focus on defensive soundness first, attacks second

Give a little to gain a lot:

Most of the time when you have top position you will be looking to restrict space between you and your opponent and keep a tight chest to chest connection to main your pin. When it's time to submit opponents however, you can often profit handsomely by giving some space for an opponent to move into. As long as you control which space is made available this will enable you to funnel your opponent's movement into whatever trap you have set. The idea of pinning is to PREVENT movement - but the idea of pinning into submission is to DIRECT movement in directions that favor you.

When the workouts done:
My students are renowned for their work ethic and I am known to push people to their maximum in training. Less well known is that I am also a big advocate of a very informal and relaxed approach to post workout dialogue as a very important counterbalance to the grind of physical training. One of the best ways to create longevity in the sport is to match the toughness of training with relaxed banter and chatting about subjects that have no relation to Jiu jitsu. I am sure all of you do the same thing. It can't all be about pressure and productivity - we all need pressure release and dialogue among friends and comrades after class is the single best way to make this part of your Jiu jitsu journey. Remember always that the path of Jiu jitsu is a long and frustrating one and the single biggest determinant of realizing your potential is STAYING POWER. Anything you can do that keeps you going longer is a blessing and nothing does that better than the venerable Jiu jitsu tradition of after class hijinks and banter. Interestingly when the Covid-19 crises hit students all told me how much they missed classes, but the single most common sentiment I got from them was that more than anything else they missed the post class camaraderie. Here I am with one of my most brilliant students and best friends, Brian Glick, talking shop and probably a few other topics well outside the shop as well. What are some of the craziest conversations and antics you get up to when the arm locks strangle are over? (Besides leg locks)

Push and pull:

If you wish to excel in Jiu jitsu there is one seemingly simple edict upon which much of your future success or failure depends - when an opponent pulls - push - and when he pushes - pull. It's a simple and well-known idea that people TALK about all the time and then forget as soon as they start sparring. Don't just SAY it - LIVE AND BREATH IT every time you're on the mat and I promise you that your performance will increase overnight. When you have a strongly resisting opponent this fundamental maxim will help your performance more than anyone technique will. Learn to take advantage of the power of your opponent's force and you will make a strong man fight HIS OWN STRENGTH as well as yours!

There's a lot more to the standing game of Jiu jitsu than takedowns:

When most people think of standing skills in Jiu jitsu they understandably think automatically in terms of takedowns. However, there are many other skills of great importance. Let's consider takedown defense for example. In Jiu jitsu a successful takedown scores two points. A strong counter to takedown that exposes an opponent's back and enables you to secure rear mount will score double that - four points. So clearly takedown defense is a potentially very profitable skill that gets widely overlooked in Jiu jitsu. Let's look at pulling guard. This is typically seen as a defeatist strategy which intent is to prevent an opponent scoring on you (usually because you believe he has superior takedown skills to you). What if we changed our thinking a little and instead of passively pulling guard, we pulled directly to a SWEEP from guard? Pulling directly to a guard sweep is no more difficult than pulling guard.

Now you can use guard pulling as a MEANS TO SCORE rather than a way to avoid being scored on. Interestingly you will score the same amount (two points) as you would have scored with a takedown. What if an opponent pulls guard on you? Most people just see this as an invitation to play the ground game. What if you saw it as an opportunity to score a quick guard passing off the pull? Now you're up three points (more than a takedown) and putting your opponent under real pressure from the start. What about instead of pulling guard you pulled directly to a submission hold? An arm lock, leg lock or strangle? Then the whole damn match would be over! You can see that there are many very potentially lucrative standing skills that get far less attention than they ought to. Perhaps you can among the first to develop these and make them a feature of your game and reap the benefits!

Looking back at yourself:

As much as I encourage students to focus on their future goals and skill development, an important part of that future focus is to periodically look back upon yourself to check for signs of progress. It can be quite a shocking experience to look back at old video of yourself in training. You can learn a lot by looking at old footage and COACHING YOUR OLD SELF. You will of course see a thousand mistakes - you know so much more now than you did then. This simple exercise will reinforce many lessons you learned and crystallize them in a memorable way to help you recall and emphasize them for future training and development. You can see potential and directions for the future. Learn to see the same potential in yourself - take a look back sometimes to help you steer the way forward.

2021 Edition

Undermining athleticism:
One of the central features of Jiu jitsu is the constant drive to UNDERMINE WHATEVER ATHLETIC POTENTIAL YOUR OPPONENT HAS. The human body is constructed in such a way that for every athletic task it is capable of performing, there is an optimal stance or bodily disposition that facilitates that task. Your goal in Jiu jitsu is to interfere with that as much as possible in order to reduce an opponent to a klutzy, tied up and useless, unathletic specimen waiting to be submitted. There are many ways to do this depending upon the situation you are in. When it comes to leg locking, arguably the most controlling means of shackling an opponent up in a manner that severely undermines his athleticism is to lace his ankles whilst holding him in cross ashi garami. That immediately prevents an opponent standing up, coming forward or scooting back and also makes turning difficult. ONCE YOU CONTROL MOVEMENT - YOU CONTROL THE GAME. Research how to restrain people and undermine their athleticism in your favorite finishing holds and watch your finishes skyrocket.

It's hard for an opponent to attack you from guard if you don't allow his feet to make effective connections to your legs and arms:
Effective attacks in Jiu jitsu are predicated upon effective grips that form connection between you and an opponent. You can use that connection to control and attack. If you can't grip and connect - you can't attack. Now guard position has two major forms of grip. The

first is the more obvious one - your hands to your opponent's body. The second is your FEET to your opponent's body (usually the legs). Your feet do almost as much grilling as your hands in Jiu jitsu. When passing, if you can shut down your opponent's ability to grip you with his feet, then you will have gone a long way towards shutting down his offense, and with his offense shut down, now you can focus on the fun stuff - passing his guard - without the distraction of being attacked as you try to pass. Seek to control his feet and prevent them making effective connections to your legs - your passing game will thank you.

The example of Georges St Pierre:
I have had the honor of coaching many truly outstanding athletes of more than two decades. None surpassed the incredible achievements of Mr. St Pierre. Everyone knows his achievements - far fewer know what it was like to train with him in the gym - yet a brief discussion of this could be very beneficial to your own progress. The first thing to note was that Mr. St Pierre was fully capable of beating the crap out of any of us any time he felt like it, but he came in to the gym only to play our game of grappling rather than fighting. He knew that grappling expertise was an important part of fighting expertise and would not try to use any of his great advantages in standing grappling and striking (or even mention them) but instead play our submission game. He would almost always pull guard and start of positions of disadvantage to remove his advantages and work on his weaknesses. His only goal was improvement in the area we were best suited to help it. If he wanted to he could have simply disengaged and stalled to avoid our strengths. He never did. He went directly into our strengths and

tried to improve his performance in those areas. He did the same thing in every boxing, Muay Thai and wrestling workout I ever saw him do. Every workout must have seemed a nightmare as it was him playing against the best people in the world in their strongest area, on their terms. If someone followed him around for a year and watched his workouts they might see him struggling the whole time - until it was fight night. Then they would see the result of all that work against specialists in their domain. Now it was time to put it all together in HIS domain - the cage - under MMA rules - and you all know how that went! DON'T FOCUS IN WINNING IN THE GYM - FOCUS ON IMPROVEMENT AND SKILL ACQUISITION - worry about WINNING when it counts - when you learn to divide those two concerns your progress will be astounding.

Grip with four appendages - not two:
When people ask me about gripping skills in Jiu jitsu they almost invariably want to talk about grip STRENGTH. Even when they talk about this they invariably refer to strength of the HANDS. Never forget that from guard position you must learn to grip with both hands AND feet. It is crucial that you develop dexterity in your feet so that they can grip and pull and push just like your hands do. The great advantage of guard position is that it UNWEIGHTS YOUR FEET so that they can be used as two extra gripping limbs. You get to fight an opponent with four of your limbs - he only gets to fight with two. Your hands are only half the story of gripping in Jiu jitsu - only when you use all four appendages in concert will you maximize your gripping potential.

Consistently Winning the little battles usually means you'll win the war:

A Jiu jitsu match is a series of little battles leading to progressively better situations until a point is reached where the opponent does not want to or cannot continue - then the war is over. This simple fact should be reflected in your training. If you want to mimic match conditions seek to win all the little battles along the way - the initial hand fights, the transition to the ground and subsequent grip fights, the battle to off balance an opponent if you're on bottom or nullify the legs if you're on top. In a competitive match these battles will go back and forth - focus on winning bad many as you can and generally the final result will go your way. Most Jiu jitsu matches are won CUMULATIVELY. Onlookers only remember the RESULT, but in truth, most of the time it was taking the majority of all those little battles for grip, angle and position that determined the outcome before the finish. Fight in the light of this truth. Don't get complacent over small battles - they all count toward the final result. Stay focused and be greedy - the more little battles you take the easier and quicker you win the overall war.

Being told two dozen details about a given move will not prove as useful to you under the pressure of sparring or competition as the three most important details ranked in order of importance. Better to remember a few items of the most important information than forget two dozen items from a forgettable and unranked list. Remember this always when both teaching and learning.

The journey from beginner to expert - physical and psychological development:

We all begin as white belts. Our common desire is to gain expertise. In physical terms it's easy to identify what changes - it is skill. When we first begin we enter as klutzes who can bare shrimp across the mat, but by the time you're a black belt you will spin effortlessly into a beautiful armbar from underneath a tough opponent without a second thought. But what about the psychological angle? What changes most from beginner to expert? Is it confidence? Do we become more confident? Not always. I know quite a few world champions who are nervous wreaks before competition or even before a hard training session. I know others who fervently believe they have inadequate skills despite winning world titles and having great renown as competitors. Is it knowledge? Not always. Some champions have vast amounts of knowledge, but others have a sparse number of moves and no interest in adding more and they are very successful at the highest levels. In my experience the single most dominant psychological trait among experts that emerged as they went from white belt to black is A CALM MIND THAT ENABLES THEM TO PROBLEM SOLVE UNDER STRESS. Almost every champion and Jiu jitsu expert I knew had this characteristic. As white belts we quickly become FRANTIC when sparring begins. Watch any beginners class and the dominant characteristic you'll see is PANIC LEADING TO ERROR AND EXHAUSTION. when you watch the black belt class you will observe extreme examples calm under stress that enables students to get out of seemingly hopeless situations and recover. Learning to develop that essential MENTAL CALM is every bit as important as developing your physical skills. Indeed, I would go so far as to say that the physical skills will prove to be of rather limited value if they are not accompanied by a mental calm that judiciously guides their use. When training don't just pay attention to the physical skills, pay attention to your state of mind.

**Every Jiu jitsu athlete tries
to create problems for their opponent.**
That's good. If you can CREATE problems faster and more imaginatively than your opponent can SOLVE them you will eventually win. But better yet is to go beyond creating PROBLEMS and create DILEMMAS. These have no solution - only a choice between two bad outcomes. When you can put opponents into dilemmas your opponent will avoid one option and will win on the other horn of the dilemma. Here Gordon Ryan demonstrates it perfectly with a front triangle combined with armbar. If his opponent stacks forward to avoid the armbar he will be strangled by the triangle. If he postures up and away from the strangle he will expose his arm to the arm bar. Whichever choice makes he will be submitted. That is the highest kind of Jiu jitsu.

**When riding the back -
 prioritize the upper body connection first:**
In Jiu jitsu you get rewarded for the back only when you sink your hooks into your opponent - no hooks - no points. It's natural to think therefore, that the hooks are the thing to focus on. While the hooks are certainly an important part of the position, it is your arms connecting your chest to your opponent's back that really enable to stay locked to a resisting opponent for extended periods of time. ONCE YOUR UPPER BODY CONNECTION IS SET, YOU CAN

ALWAYS WORK YOUR WAY INTO LOWER BODY HOOKS. Ultimately you will need both upper and lower body connection to succeed from the back - but if circumstances mean that for a period of time you can only have one - choose upper body.

Four vs two:
One of the primary motivations to use open guard positions is that you can fight with four of your limbs while your opponent can only use two against you. He gets two (weaker) limbs along with the mobility advantage of being on his feet and the weight/pressure of gravity as his weapons. You as the guard player get four limbs (including the two strongest). This is the essential nature of the battle. You have different weapons but both are excellent - you have to learn how to use those different weapons to advantage. Learning to see the difference and use it to your advantage is a key part of winning the eternal battle between guard vs guard passer.

There is a direct correlation between how long you can stay on the back and the number of strangles you can score on the back:
Submissions takes take time. Strangles from the back take even more time than usual. If you can't maintain back position for a respectable amount of time it's going to be very difficult to reliably finish from there. As such you have to develop your back-riding ability as a skill in itself. Only when you can MAINTAIN the back position can you FINISH from the back position. Begin by seeing how long you can stay on a tough training partners back. Try to

improve your times with every attempt. Train your eyes to SEE submission opportunities but don't act on them until you've held the position as long as you aimed to do. Time spent training this way will pay big dividends when you have to go against an opponent with good defensive skills and where the finishes don't come easy.

Less contact - less effectiveness:
Jiu jitsu is the art and science of establishing physical connection with an opponent that enables you to control their movement more than they can control yours and use that control to steer them towards submission. The more contact and connection they can establish on you when they are in good position, the more trouble they can create for you. Accordingly, a big part of the game is that of denying connection and contact when it does not suit you. When you are working in a talented opponents guard, try to deny him useful connection whilst establishing your own. His primary connectors are his feet and lower legs. If you control and monitor those you make his game quite difficult. Learning to distinguish between contact and connection that is beneficial and that which is hazardous is a big part of your development.

Breaking stance and posture:
 Most Jiu jitsu students are made aware of the critical importance of stance and posture early in their training. You soon learn that breaking an opponent's stance and posture pays big dividends in sparring. Perhaps the most impressive example of this is the one

used the least - breaking an opponent's stance and posture while attacking him with a submission hold. It's bad enough to get caught in a tight submission hold - it's TWICE as bad to get caught in a tight submission and then get your stance and posture broken down so that you cannot even defend yourself properly. Remember that submission defense almost always requires some kind of defensive posture - if you lose that then the hold becomes practically indefensible. Next time you are attacking a submission hold - GO THE EXTRA DISTANCE AND LOOK TO BREAK THE OPPONENT'S STANCE AND POSTURE AS WELL - you will soon find far fewer opponents are escaping your favorite holds.

Details and direction:
Jiu jitsu is absolutely a detail-oriented sport. Moves that are performed 90% correctly will fail when used against someone your own level. Adherence to Small details is very often the difference between gold medal and empty hands at the end of a competition. Nonetheless, you must recognize that progress is not only about accumulating details on moves. You must have those details ENCASED IN A GENERAL SENSE OF DIRECTION. You must always have a sense of purpose when you play Jiu jitsu - the details are the means of exhibiting that sense of purpose/direction. In truth you can only remember so many details under stress. Better to have a smaller number of highly relevant details shrouded in a strong sense of direction than endless numbers of details that you can barely remember. For example, in guard passing. A general sense of purpose is conveyed by a principle "seek to create pressure by moving side to side and favor passing to the side opposite the direction your opponent's knees are pointing" and this can give you

a broad sense of purpose. Then you can fill in the details of exactly how best to do this with details of grip, body positioning, stance etc. So yes - accumulate details over time and do your best to remember them all, but remember that they will serve you much better when they are subsumed under broad guidelines that give you the big picture of what you ought to on the macro level while the details guide you on the micro level.

It's not so much a game
of making yourself faster and stronger than the other guy, so much as it's a game of using restraints and broken posture to make the other guy weaker and slower than yourself. Strong men can be made weak by forcing them into unnatural and broken postures. Fast men can be rendered slow by restraints and obstacles. In Jiu jitsu, as much as we extol gaining strength for ourselves, we venerate robbing an opponent of strength even more.

Knowing what success feels like and what failure feels like - minimum requirements for submission holds:
Submission holds are an all or nothing affair. Typically, they either work completely and end the match or don't work at all and the action continues (occasionally there are cases where they work but the opponent just keeps fighting on with a broken limb and in these cases, they have worked to some degree insofar as the rest of the match will be easier fighting against a partially crippled opponent). They take up a considerable amount of energy when applied full

force against a tough opponent. You definitely don't want to hang on grimly to a failed submission hold that has little or no chance of working and needlessly expend vast sums of precious energy fruitlessly. On the other hand, you don't want to quit early at the first sign of resistance and lose a great chance to win. How do you distinguish scenarios where we should cut our losses and release to go on to something else versus holding on to get the win? The key is to recognize the minimum essential features to the success of the move - for example every heel hook requires that at a minimum your opponent's knee should be trapped within your knee line. Every juji gatame requires at the minimum that your hips should be locked to an opponent's shoulder/armpit. Every Kimura has the minimum requirement that your figure four lock should be above your opponent's elbow. That minimum requirement(s) is your basic guide. If you satisfy it - it is probably a good idea to persist with the lock. If you can't satisfy it - it's probably a good idea to abandon it and move on to another attack. Know your minimum requirements and you will know ahead of time whether success or failure with the hold in imminent and save yourself a lot frustration.

The undisputed king of positions - the back:
As much as I love leg locks and arm locks, if I could only have one submission for the rest of my life I would choose strangles from the back without hesitation. Indeed, it is no exaggeration to see you could build an EXTREMELY effective style of Jiu jitsu that had absolutely no leg locks, no arm locks, no guillotine, Darce, strangles etc. only a rear strangles. It would be equally effective Gi and no Gi, grappling and fighting, standing or ground, sport and self-defense. You can get the back from anywhere. You can use scrambles to the

back when guard passing, as a counter to most leg locks, at the completion of any sweep or takedown, as a follow on from any pin. You could become a dominant world champion with the rear strangle as your only submission hold provided your positional game was up to the task of reliably getting you to the back. Thankfully we don't have to make the choice of a single submission and so we can learn a bunch of them to make the game easier, but still, lesson learned - study your pathways to the back and your finishes from there - it will never let you down in any scenario in which you may find yourself.

Guard position -The cycle of push and pull:

In most cases the basic cycle of guard position is PUSH FOR DEFENSE - PULL FOR OFFENSE. In the majority of cases (there are obvious exceptions) this holds true. Whenever some is close to passing our guard our first reaction is to PUSH and create space to recover our feet and knees. Whenever we want to bring an opponent forward into submissions or sweeps in a forward direction we PULL (pushing sweeps to the rear are the exception). Learning to cycle between pushing and pulling - offense and defense - is one of the fundamental skills of the sport. Your feet and knees, hands and elbows will be your primary pushers and pullers. Learning to use them in a team in opposing directions based upon what is unfolding second by second in a match will be one of your greatest areas of study. The switch from defense to offense back to defense happens very quickly and the better you and your opponent's get, the faster it will have to be.

The spine/head is the longest lever in the human body –
use it from bottom position: The first guard you learn in Jiu jitsu is usually closed guard. Often, I think this common practice is an error - Closed guard probably should not be the first guard you learn - it's actually a very specialized position that does not always come smoothly from the pin escapes that students learn first in jitsu. I often think half guard and variations of open guard may be better guards for beginning students to learn first. Nonetheless closed guard is an extremely important guard to learn whether you learn it first or last or somewhere in between. Understand immediately that there is going to be a contest between you and your opponent for posture. You want to break him forward - he wants to stay upright and away. It will come down to the pull of your legs and stomach versus the pull up and away of his back and head. Who wins? As always - THE ONE WHO USES THE LEVER TO ADVANTAGE. Your opponent's spine is a long lever. If the lock of your closed guard is low - at the base of the lever - your pull will be weak and unlikely to break a good opponent's posture. If you shift the lock of your feet higher - up to the head and shoulders - you are operating at the end of the lever and your pulling force will be considerable. When you want to pull - get your feet and legs up high on the back. Much of your success with arm bars, triangles and omoplatas will come out of your ability to switch to a high lock from closed guard - practice it constantly until it is natural and easy for you.

You can do it!
One of the most common questions I am asked is whether you can come back from injury and perform well in Jiu jitsu. It's natural to doubt your ability to come back from a major setback. Around

February 2nd 2019 Gordon Ryan fought a tough match against the great João Gabriel Rocha. About halfway through the match he completely tore his LCL off the bone He was able to hold on and win a very close match but the damage was done. He was scheduled for reconstructive surgery and told that it would probably be a year until he was back to normal. This was tragic news as 2019 was a n ADCC World Championship year - missing the worlds would be a terrible blow to any elite grappler. Initially he could not train at all. The only form of training was mental knowledge training. He would come to class and simply watch from the sidelines to keep his mind in the game. This went in for months. Early tests showed he was regaining linear mobility quite well, but the kind of inward and outward joint mobility required for Jiu jitsu just wasn't there. Finally, he got cleared for light training. The early sessions were not very encouraging. He was a late to every move and often I could see him struggling to perform even basic moves. There are few things more frustrating to a Jiu Jitsu player than knowing what you are supposed to do, but being physically incapable of doing it. Eight weeks out from ADCC I fully assumed he would not be going to the World Championships - he just wasn't at that level. I was planning the team performance around the other athletes and was assuming Gordon would be a useful training partner for the competitors but not competing himself. One day Mr. Ryan came in and had a very good workout. He performed several of his favorite moves very well. Next day he looked even better. By the end of the week he was beating everyone in the gym. At four weeks he repeatedly and easily finished a famous visiting athlete - it was obvious - he was back in the game. Four weeks later he went to give one of the greatest performances in ADCC history - there will never be a shortage of people counting you out - just make sure you yourself are never one of them.

How much are you using your head when you grapple?

Usually when we say "use your head" we mean you ought to use your brain more - but in grappling it very often is used literally. The head is one of the most effective tools you have in grappling, particularly when your hands are preoccupied (which is almost always the case). The most important function of the head is as a pushing implement - though it can other functions as well. Whenever your hands are busy and you need to push, block or trap a part of an opponent's body - USE YOUR HEAD. It will often mean the difference between a move working or failing. Look how Gordon Ryan uses his head to flatten and align an opponent as his hands are preoccupied by a body lock pass grip. Keep a straight spine to minimize neck strain as you do it - you will be delighted at how often and how effectively you can use your head to supplement the pushing, blocking and wedging of your arms.

Watching Jiu jitsu:

Whenever my students are injured I usually encourage them to come in periodically and watch classes from the sideline. Why? When you can't train your body - train your MIND. Remember always that the mind governs our actions. You want a faster game in Jiujitsu? That will require a mind that can process options faster just as much as a faster body. The problem is that when most people watch Jiu jitsu they FOLLOW the action rather than try to JUDGE and ANTICIPATE the action. They look only at the RESULT rather than the PROCESSES that brought about the results. When you watch, picture yourself out there and ask yourself second by second what you would be doing in their stead. How you would respond to other fellows' attacks and defenses. Get engaged when you watch. The mental workout is every bit as useful and productive as the physical one the athletes on the mat are having.

Back up buddy:
There are many ways to get hurt in combat sports but one of the most unnecessary comes in situations where two athletes are sparring in a crowded room and crash into another couple of athletes sparring next to them. This kind of incident is usually dismissed as part of the game and laughed off. I never took this approach. In the heyday of the blue basement when Georges St Pierre was getting ready for a big MMA show or the squad was getting ready for ADCC we would often have well over a hundred people working out in a class. In this type of situation, it is absolutely crucial that everyone in the room have a good sense of where they are on the mat relative to the people around them. Nothing is more frustrating than an athlete getting ready for a show and getting injured with a cut from an elbow or a joint injury from someone rolling into their arm or leg at an inopportune time - I have myself been knocked out cold twice from heel kicks to the back of the head while sparring next to athletes whose enthusiasm exceeded their sense of distancing. When you start getting close to other people - make a point of quickly and fluidly rolling away from them and start where you left off. Keep a sense of your surroundings. I teach this in terms of self-defense training - just as tunnel vision can be a very dangerous thing in self-defense scenarios, so too it can be dangerous in a crowded training room. Train yourself to pay attention as you

grapple in training and it will help you pay attention to your surroundings if you have to defend yourself outside the dojo. There are more than enough ways in Jiu jitsu to get injured without adding this easily avoided method to the list. Students - be the one who keeps awareness of your surroundings and does not injure or annoy those around you. Teachers - run a tight ship. Make students aware of the potential danger of collision and build a culture in your dojo that takes pride in being professional and courteous and I promise you your injury rate will drop and class camaraderie will increase.

Young masters:
One of the great cliches of martial arts is that old masters have vast reservoirs of knowledge that younger athletes don't and therefore that younger athletes may be very good in competition but won't be very good as teachers until presumably they become much older and then they become great teachers. This is complete hogwash. What counts in Jiu jitsu wisdom is not your physical age but rather your accumulated time on the mat and the quality of that time. For example, I would much rather be instructed by a twenty-year-old who had trained every day from an early age and who was totally immersed in the sport and studied everything from fundamentals to cutting edge material and logged an impressive fifteen thousand hours on the mats than a fifty-five-year-old who trained once a week and who had only logged around four thousand hours of mat time. When it comes to knowledge accumulated mat time is a far more reliable indicator of knowledge than physical age. Add to that the quality of mat time - depth of study, ability to articulate that knowledge to others, degree to which experimentation and research was performed over that mat time etc. - and this is what will tell you

is the degree of expertise they possess, not their age. I am constantly amazed at the teaching prowess of my young students, Garry Tonon, Gordon Ryan, Craig Jones and Nicky Ryan have a depth of knowledge that would deeply impress the older generations in the sport. Remember that Sir Isaac Newton and Albert Einstein revolutionized the world with their knowledge in their early twenties - no one tried to dismiss their ideas because they were young. Martial arts are no different. There are young masters who have built incredible stores of knowledge that can change your game.

Teaching:

Most of what I write about is about your goal of LEARNING Jiu jitsu. However, a big part of my approach to learning is getting my students involved in TEACHING. There is a great relationship between the acts of learning and teaching and as you progress in one you will inevitably improve at the other. I often get my students to teach moves back to me in class or to teach some innovation they have figured out. The act of teaching forces you to figure out the most important details and features of a technique. Asking yourself how to present the information makes you understand the technique more clearly. Presenting it in a way that is understandable for all levels makes you prioritize the most pertinent details. Obviously, it's easier to teach to others when you've reached a higher level in the sport, but start early. Start by teaching friends at the same level as you some aspect of the game you have researched and try it out together. Make adjustments in accordance with the problems you encounter. Just the act of asking the important questions and understanding the central problems involved around the technique can enhance your understanding. It works wonders for my students both as athletes and as teachers themselves. Teaching is a skill like any other, and, like any skill, the best people are usually those who start early and do it often. I started teaching when I was a blue belt in the late 1990's. Nothing makes me happier as a teacher than seeing my students' breakdown complex material and improve the understanding and knowledge of those who train around them. It makes everyone in the room part of a project and gives a whole new meaning to their training. Try it. Start small with friends and see how it can benefit your game.

Loneliness in a crowded room:
 Jiu jitsu is at the same time both a deeply personal and a very group-oriented journey. You train and develop in a group - but you experience everything, every small daily triumph and failure, as an individual. In truth there will be many more failures than there will be triumphs. It's natural to feel that everyone else is stronger, faster and more talented than you. That everyone else learns and progresses faster than you do. Don't get too caught up in comparisons with those around you. Focus more on comparisons with earlier renditions of yourself. As long as you continue to improve a little at a time you will get to the level you want. You will get there faster than some and slower than others. It does not really matter WHEN you get there so much as it matters THAT you get there. It's good to be ambitious and want to get to goals quickly and efficiently but temper this sentiment with a healthy dose of reality. If everyone else in the room is progressing at roughly the same rate as you then you will never suddenly feel as though the game suddenly became easy. Remember also that the only common

characteristic that everyone who got to a high level in the sport exhibited as PERSISTENCE. When it gets lonely and disheartening take a step back and reflect on the virtue of persistence. Understand that everyone else who entered that room felt the same way many, many times. Most, quit and so never realized their potential in this domain. The few that didn't are the one who are so good they make you feel as you do know. Stay in the game. The feeling of frustration that is so strong in you today can be replaced by elation tomorrow with just one small and unexpected success.

It can't all be hard work and suffering:
Sometimes visitors to our gym are rather surprised by the amount of banter and wisecracking there is before and after class. I'm very much in favor of this. When it's time to work - work hard - but when it's over it's important to have some fun (usually at each other's expense). Overly formal atmospheres always felt a little uncomfortable to me. I always disliked titles like "Professor" or even worse "master." I always felt that an informal and relaxed atmosphere that nonetheless had a clear sense of when it was time to knuckle down and get the hard work done and when it was ok to joke around got the right balance of industry and relaxation that made training in a tough sport enjoyable. Some of my favorite memories in Jiu jitsu came from times AFTER class and that's a healthy thing as laughter and fun have probably brought more students back for tomorrow's workout than workouts ever did. Just make sure it doesn't degenerate into comedy when you're supposed to be doing the hard work - but once the final round is done there is as much benefit in laughter as there is in technique.

Joint locks - don't be in a hurry to extend the limb:

There are two ways to submit an opponent in Jiu jitsu - strangles and joint locks. Overall, I believe strangles are the more effective of the two but joint locks are still a truly vital part of the game. You must make a deep study of the skill of attacking the arms and legs of an opponent. Probably the single most common problem I see in developing students who have gotten into a position to joint lock an opponent is AN UNNECESSARY RUSH TO COMPLETION that sacrifices control and allows an opponent to escape. When it comes to joint locks CONTROL BEATS SPEED. There are exceptions to this. There are times when a fast entry and finish can get you a win before an opponent can get into a defensive reaction - but for every time you see this happen you will see twenty cases where too much concern with speed weakens your control and you end up with nothing. Focus on a tight connection to the joint above the joint that you are attacking. If you are attacking the knee - get a good connection to the hip. If your attacking the elbow, get a good connection to the shoulder. Don't be afraid to move with your opponent to maintain that connection. When you feel the connection is strong and you can control your opponent's movement - THEN go to attack the joint. Victory will go to the athlete who exhibits great control more often than the athlete who exhibits great speed.

Are you ready for the next move?

If there is one certainty in Jiu jitsu it is that the majority of your attempted moves will fail. This is a simple reflection of the fact that your opponent knows the same moves you do and also the counters. Given the prevalence of failure it is crucial that you have mapped out what to do the moment you feel that the move has failed and recovery is not possible. We all spend our Jiu jitsu lives seeking to achieve success, but in reality, the smart way to approach things is to seek to recover and exploit failure since this is far more common than success. Here Nicky Ryan has lost control of his opponents' knee - a clear sign that this heel hook/knee bar attempt has failed beyond recovery - the only question now is where to go from here. If you are asking the question now - it's already too late. You must train yourself to ask it before that critical moment.

First contact - hands or feet?

Grappling is all about connection. No connection to an opponent means no grappling. At some you have to come to grips to make the action start. When you first come to make grips from open guard you have a choice between feet and hands. In truth, much of that choice will be determined by your opponent. If he positions himself in certain ways - hands will make more sense - in others - feet will make more sense. Whenever he denies you one, the other will be available. Generally, in no Gi you will initially use your feet to establish contact at the ankles and knees. Hands at the wrists, elbows and collar. Just as you test water with a single hand or foot before jumping in, so too, test an opponent with a single hand or foot before jumping in to full connection.

Class is never really over:

Its natural when you've just finished a tough class to want to get the hell out of the dojo and head somewhere less strenuous. Note however, that the time immediately after class is probably the time when you have the most honest and realistic assessments of your ability and flaws as you still have the feelings of exasperation and frustration at failed moves and the memory of exactly what they were. There is no better time therefore to puzzle out a problem than after class. Often my students come to me with problems right after a rough day of sparring. Sometimes I have answers based on my similar experiences from years ago - sometimes I don't - that's fine - then it's time to experiment and figure it out. The feeling of finishing a tough workout is good, but the feeling of finishing a tough workout AND knowing what you need to do to perform better tomorrow is even better. Use that time immediately after class - it's a great time for improvement.

Escapes - testing yourself:

Here is a moment when my students and I were teaching a seminar in Singapore. Much of what we went over was concerned with escapes from bad position. When it comes time to escape the mount no gi, I strongly favor the kipping escape. This is an escape that superficially looks like a push, but really it is based upon the kipping action of the legs (kipping is a movement of the legs designed to create momentum in a given direction - most commonly used when people want to cheat doing pull ups to make it easier to get up to the bar but also very useful when you want to make it easier to escape certain pins), along with misdirection of your opponent's lines of resistance. All of my students excel at this move, in fact there were times early in their careers I had to tell them to stop using it so much because they were going into competitions and deliberately putting themselves in the bottom mount position so they could simply escape and heel hook unwitting opponents! Here Gordon Ryan demonstrates during the seminar. Note the ease of execution and the changes in direction as the move unfolds. In my upcoming NEW WAVE JIU JITSU - ESCAPES video I will cover this fascinating method and show its link to counter offense where you can escape directly into strong leg lock attacks so that you don't only get out - you finish the opponent as you do so. When you get really good you can get fancy and perform the escape with one arm as Gordon Ryan does here. All of my students training begins with defense. Having the confidence that comes from knowing that you can escape the worst positions and counter attack is worth its weight in gold.

Identify the problem:
Every submission hold has an escape. Every escape involves a set of movements - but invariably there is ONE movement that does the majority of the work of escape. For example, in upper body submission holds from guard involving your legs such as triangle, juji gatame arm bar, omoplata etc. - most of the early escapes are postural escapes involving your opponent's HEAD rising away from you to create distance and this is the core of the escape/defense overall. Once you understand this as the athlete trying to perform the submission it's all a matter of building increasingly powerful HEAD CONTROL as the basis of your submission game from guard.

Focus upon the most pressing problem pays big dividends in Jiu jitsu. In a word of ten thousand problems learning to focus on the biggest ones first makes a big difference to your performance. Under stress it's much easier to solve one bigger problem than a dozen smaller ones simultaneously. Develop a clear idea of what the biggest threat to your success is and attack that threat relentlessly - you will soon notice the difference in your performance.

The interplay of push and pull:
When playing bottom position in Jiu-jitsu there is a continual battle for DISTANCE CONTROL that leads to a never-ending interplay between PUSHING and PULLING. From guard we always seek an optimum distance that keeps an opponent at a range that gives us SUFFICIENT ROOM TO ATTACK (space creation) and yet at the same time SUFFICIENT PROXIMITY TO ATTACK (space restriction). In short, if the opponent is too close you won't have room to move into your attacks. If he is too far away you won't be able to get and main connection to attack. We need to seek a middle distance we're the opponent is close enough to attack yet not so close that we our attacks get stifled. As such you must be able to PUSH BACK WITH FRAMES if he gets too close, and PULL HIM CLOSE WITH GRIPS if he is far away. Because things happen very quickly you must be able to switch from pull to push and back again at a moment's notice. As a general rule DEFENSE IS BUILT AROUND PUSHING and OFFENSE IS BUILT AROUND PULLING although there are some important exceptions to this general rule. Best of all are grips and positions that enable you to do both - such as ashi garami. Next time you play guard pay more attention to push and pull dynamics. When opponents threaten to

pass - FOCUS ON STRONG PUSHING FRAMES. When opponents hand back FOCUS ON PULLING THEM INTO YOUR ATTACKS. It will make your developing guard game progress rapidly.

**The more dominant your grips and position -
the more you take your time when moving:**
Sometimes Jiu jitsu rewards us for moving quickly - usually when we don't have any form of advantage over our opponent. In these cases, an advantage in speed may be the only advantage you have and if you can get to the next position ahead of your opponent you can profit. Sometimes Jiu jitsu rewards use for being slow. This is usually when you have a dominant grip and (usually top) position. In these cases, time is your friend. Time spent in these positions is tiring and frustrating for an opponent. As he works harder and harder to get out, the more risks he will have to take to escape and the more likely he will leave a limb behind to be taken. So next time you take a dominating position/grip - take your time! Don't be in such a rush for your next move. Remember that WHEN YOU HAVE NO CONTROL TIME IS YOUR ENEMY - BUT WHEN YOU HAVE CONTROL - TIME IS YOUR FRIEND.

Control the hips:
 The only scoring position from the back in Jiu Jitsu is rear mount. This involves hooking your two legs into your opponent's hips. There are many other back controls that don't involve the legs at all. They don't score but are nonetheless very useful methods of control

that can win matches. My favorite involves the use of tight waist grips that offer direct control of an opponent's hip with an arm. It does a fine job of giving you hip to hip connection along with a great ability to off balance an opponent and leaves you with a free arm that can be put anywhere in response to rapid changes as the match unfolds. When you don't have hooks in - throw in a tight waist grip as an excellent means of dynamic control.

Taking yourself to a new level – front headlocks and the example of Craig Jones:

At any given time, our game is certain level. This can change a little week by week depending upon training conditions and the state of our body, but there is a rough level that can be roughly measured by your skill set/knowledge and how you stack up against other athletes in sparring/competition. Once you can to a level that you find satisfactory it's natural to take stock of yourself and see yourself as having a certain type of game. Both you and Your classmates have a good idea of what your strengths and weaknesses are. You see yourself as being good at moves A, B and C but not very interested in E and F. You take that skill set of yours and refine it a little and that's you. You can do pretty well with this approach - but you will never reach your potential. You have to periodically set projects to add whole new aspects to your game. This is the only way to avoid stagnation over time. Take the example of Craig Jones. Early in his career he was known primarily for his triangle attacks. When he came to America to compete in EBI events he realized he had to excel in the leg lock game. He took that project on with such gusto that he became known as one of the best in the world. Not satisfied, he went on to develop a very powerful back attack in response to opponents who ran from the pressure of his leg game. Watching his development a few years ago I talked with him about the need to develop a powerful front headlock/Guillotine game as a counter to opponents who did not want to engage his dangerous submissions game or who were faster than him in a scramble. Immediately he took the project on. Within a short time, he was developing lethal variations of Guillotines, anacondas and Darce strangles. Then tying this back to his already formidable back game and leg game. Now he has one of the best front headlock games I've ever seen! THIS is how you keep developing. NEVER SEE YOURSELF AS A COMPLETED PROJECT. Rather than cover up and hide your weaknesses - train them to become your new strengths and ally them to your old strengths.

Your legs vs his head:
One of the basic features of Jiu jitsu is the notion of controlling greater strength and aggression with lesser strength and aggression via mechanical and tactical advantage. One of the surest ways to do this is to use the strongest parts of the human body (legs and hips) against the weaker parts (head and shoulders for example). Two excellent examples of this would be the triangle and juji gatame arm bar - both of which directly match your legs against an opponent's head and arm. Whenever possible look for this kind of match up in your favor. IF YOU ARE TO DEFEAT BIGGER AND STRONGER OPPONENTS THEN YOU MUST SEEK TO FIGHT YOUR OPPONENTS UPPER BODY WITH YOUR LOWER BODY AS MUCH AS POSSIBLE. If you make it a battle of your upper body against a similarly skilled and bigger opponents' upper body it is unlikely you will win. MAKE IT A FIGHT BETWEEN YOUR

LOWER BODY AND HIS UPPER BODY AND VICTORY WILL FIND A PATH TO YOUR DOOR OFTEN.

The ultimate submission:
We all have our favorite submission holds - in time I hope you develop at least five to six submissions that you can attack from anywhere on anyone - but never lose sight of a fundamental truth in grappling - the ultimate submission is not a hold per se - it is FATIGUE. If you can PHYSICALLY AND MENTALLY BREAK an opponent with fatigue he will submit with his MIND first and then with his BODY second. A big part of your skill set has to be the skill of WEARING DOWN AND EXHAUSTING AN OPPONENT SO THAT ALL THE SUBMISSION HOLDS ARE EASY TO APPLY AND TO WHICH AN OPPONENT WILL GLADLY SURRENDER. There are ways to control and manipulate grips, stance and pace that are heavily in your favor so that an opponent is working at two or three times the rate you are. If you can maintain this the result is inevitable - an opponent who is looking for an excuse to quit - your submission hold provides that excuse. When you put hands on an opponent your constant underlying goal should be to create a disparity in work rate skewed in your favor that opens the door to submission later in the match.

Showdown in Texas tomorrow night:
Tomorrow night In Austin Texas for WNO grappling. Squad seniors Gordon Ryan and Craig Jones will take on two extremely talented

opponents. In the co main event Gordon Ryan will take on Jiu jitsu dynamo Roberto Jiménez - one of the most talented of the new generation Jiu jitsu players. They have battled each other in the gym before and it was a war! The stage always adds something to the equation so this should be a fascinating match where they both know what they have to do to beat each other based on past experience and the one who finds their path onstage will take it. In the main event Australian grappling superstar Craig Jones takes on a surging star among the new generation Jiu jitsu athletes - Ronaldo Jr - who has been tearing up the competition scene recently. He is one of the fastest men in Jiu jitsu, very difficult to control. He is a star member of team ATOS, so you know he will be very well prepared and in tremendous shape. They always do a good job of sending their athletes out in peak condition and with a well worked out strategy. Both are fascinating match ups. I have always said that there are two main ways to excel in Jiu jitsu. You can either make yourself a master of movement and make movement your weapon; or you can make yourself a master of preventing movement and make control your weapon. Mr. Ryan and Mr. Jones are both true masters of CONTROLLING movement - but both of their opponents are masters of CREATING movement - so this will be a fascinating clash of styles! Weigh in is tonight here in Austin and then tomorrow night Flo Grappling will broadcast the action - I hope you enjoy the show!!

Victory in Texas!!

Craig Jones and Gordon Ryan both won brilliant submission victories against very tough opponents tonight here in Austin Texas. Gordon Ryan took on the very talented Roberto Jiménez. He expressed a desire in training to avoid using leg locks and focus on arm bar from mount as the means to victory. He released an early leg lock and focused on passing to mount and juji gatame arm-bars. His first attempt was close but Mr. Jiménez escapes brilliantly under pressure. The second attempt however was devastating and secured the win. Craig Jones took on the brilliant ATOS emerging star Ronaldo Jr. Both men went immediately to their strengths, Craig Jones with his extremely dangerous open guard and Ronaldo Jr with his speedy passing skills. After some strong exchanges Mr. Jones latched on to an ashi garami and converted to a 50/50 variation. After a brief fight for hand control and heel exposure Mr. Jones got into a powerful breaking position and won another great victory. Both athletes showed their incredible mastery of the squad ideal of control that leads to submission. Now it's time to return to Puerto Rico and get everyone ready for new challenges! Hope you all enjoyed the show!

Back home in Puerto Rico!

It was great to back in the gym today training the juniors for upcoming competitions. As much as I love travel there is a true pleasure in getting back to home ground and into a routine that builds the skills you need to excel. Thank you all so much for the interest you show the squads development and growth. It was so impressive to see Craig Jones and Gordon Ryan show the skills we work every day on the mat so perfectly in competition. No technique, strategy or set of tactics is a completed project however - so as always, it's back to the mat to refine and improve what you have and discover what you don't!

Getting under an opponent's center of gravity is the key to any lifting throw or sweep:

sweeps come in different forms - some are trips, some are like wrestling takedowns, some involve getting behind the opponent. The biggest and most impressive looking sweeps are those where you get under an opponent and lift - these create amplitude and flip an opponent over straight to his back. It's important to focus on two things. First, get under your opponent. Second, keep contact with the floor with the other foot and your same side shoulder so that you can create drive off the floor and create power out of your lifting position. When you can do this, you can get the kind of amplitude you see Gordon Ryan exhibit here at the World Championships.

Plot your next move:

There are times in Jiu jitsu where you have to move quickly and keep moving - there simply isn't time to think and you have to trust in the habits you gained through training in the gym to prevail. Fortunately, there are just as many times where you DO have time to stop, think and plot your next move among competing options. Unfortunately, we all have the tendency to ignore the different nature of these two situations and we often just unthinkingly charge ahead to the next move when we actually had plenty of time to think and plot. MAKE SURE YOU USE TIME CONSTRUCTIVELY IF TIME IS AVAILABLE - it often means the difference between moving for the sake of moving versus moving with a purpose. There are many situations in Jiu jitsu where you exert sufficient control where you can take some time to figure out the next move.

Only one position truly merges position and submission - the back:

If you look at the pins of Jiu jitsu you will see that as desirable as they are - you still have quite a bit of work to do to go beyond the pin into the submission. Getting side pin or mounted or north south or knee on belly is good, but getting the arm or neck from there requires a significant set of skills. The rear mount on the other hand leaves you VERY close to submission. Unless your opponent has good defensive skills a simple wrapping of your arm around the neck is enough to end it. You can see how closely the position (rear mount) is to the submission (rear strangle) by the fact that the escape from one entails the escape from the other. This is not true for say, a mounted arm bar or Kimura from side or knee on belly. Usually escaping the pin is one thing, the submission from that pin is another. As such rear mount/rear strangle is the single best synthesis of position and submission in the sport. Mastering the art of getting there, staying there and finishing from there is the best way to close the gap between position and submission in your game.

Open guard knees to chest:

People talk about posture all the time in Jiu jitsu - understand from the start that different situations will require different postures from you to maximize your efficiency. When it comes to open guard

- if you do not have a controlling grip on your opponent - be sure to KEEP YOUR KNEES CLOSE TO YOUR CHEST. This lessens the chance of an opponent explosively clearing your legs and passing before you can react. It also lessens the danger of a quick leg lock entry by the top player. In short - it makes you DEFENSIVELY SOUND at all times until you can get a solid grip upon your opponent that allows you to focus on offense.

Priorities:
Any time you're in a bad situation it is imperative that you prioritize the most serious threats first and address them before the secondary threats. Any time you are in a bad spot in Jiu jitsu you will face multiple threats. Some will be more serious than others - make sure those are the first ones you address. Bad position is already bad enough without making it even worse by mistakenly trying to deal with secondary threats before primary threats.

Working the sidelines:
The best place to train in the room is of course, out on the mat. However, life has a way of taking us off the mat, injury for example. When this happens, the next best place is the sideline - training your mind. When most people sit on the sideline and watch it's for the purpose of ENTERTAINMENT. That's fine, but you can do much better than that - watch for the purpose of gaining KNOWLEDGE. When you watch, imagine yourself as one of the people on the mat. Try to give better responses to the second by second action than the

person you observe. What is he doing? What would you do better? Why is your recommended course of action better than his? Done this way you become an active MENTAL participant in their PHYSICAL struggle. Doing this will make your mental game very sharp and make the task of coming back to the physical game much easier.

Breaking balance:

People will tell you all the time about the power of body weight to create pressure from top position. What they often overlook is that you can use the opponents body weight against HIM from BOTTOM just as easily as he can use it against YOU from TOP - if you can break his balance. From the top players perspective his weight is both a blessing and curse. If he can maintain his balance he can use his weight to immobilize, crush and fatigue you. If he can't maintain his balance his weight will make him stumble and extend himself. The whole game then, becomes one of balance. As a bottom player if you regularly make an opponent stumble reach for the floor - half the game is won. The time immediately after a stumble - where an opponent tries desperately to regain his posture and position, is one of the most vulnerable. Attacks that normally seem very difficult suddenly become very easy. The surest sign that an attack on an opponent's balance has been successful is his hips or hands involuntarily touching the mat. Practice knocking an opponent down to hips and hands as often as you can.

How good are you at getting out of bad positions?

Whenever people ask me to diagnose their skill level one of the first things I observe is their skill at getting out of bad positions. Why? Because that will tell me not only how good they are DEFENSIVELY but also OFFENSIVELY. This might strike you as strange. How can defensive skill reflect your offensive skill? Simple - the more faith you have in your defense the more risks you will take with your offense. Your success will always be determined by the amount of risk you are willing to subject yourself to. As they say - NOTHING RISKED, NOTHING GAINED. If you won't take the risk associated with offense you'll never even begin an attack. If you're afraid that when you try to attack you may be open to positional counters that leave you pinned in holds from which you can't escape - then you won't take the risk of attacking. The only thing that will liberate you from those fears that hold you back is the belief that you can escape any hold. The moment you believe that you will attack and hold nothing back.

Going beyond pinning:

The basic theme of Jiu jitsu is of getting to dominant upper body pins to gain positional advantage. To actually SUBMIT someone however, you'll need to do more than pin them - YOU WILL NEED TO ISOLATE A LIMB. Learning to isolate and control a limb from a dominant pin is the bridge between position and submission. Whenever you get to a pin in training don't be satisfied with the points you've scored. Go further and isolate a limb - that is the only way you will be able to submit opponents.

Gripping from guard is very different from most scenarios:
When people talk about gripping skills they usually mean gripping with the HANDS. In fact, in Jiu jitsu we can play guard position with four limbs not two. You will be expected to form connection with hand AND feet. All your life you have learned to contour your hand to maximize grip. Now you must learn the same again with your feet. The key is to CONTOUR your feet around the target - just as you do with your hands. If you want to PULL with your feet, we generally use your shoelaces and retract our toes. If you want to PUSH - use the sole of the foot. Learning to grip Qi the tour feet from guard is one of the first skills that pertains to the Jiu jitsu game.

Don't give it away for free (unless you're setting a trap):
The grip fighting that precedes engagement is a subtle art. Too often athletes give free access to good grips to their opponents. If he gets a good grip on you from which to begin the process of control to attack then it should be because he EARNED it - not because you gave it to him. When he goes to control your wrist, pull your wrist away or strip his grip and take your own - don't just leave wrists out there to be taken and controlled. The only exception to this is when you are setting traps for an opponent and you are using a bait to draw him in. If grip is the first step to control and control is what leads to match winning submission - then make sure he never gets easy grips that lead you into a downward spiral. Be ready deny, block and strip grips because the moment they are established a good opponent will be looking to take them further.

When the work is done:
One of the clearest signs that you have a sustainable training environment is the clarity of the division between work time and playtime in the training. When it's go time, everyone has to be all in. No bullshit, all focus - you're there to be the best athlete you can. But when it's done there has to be some clown time to make it an enjoyable part of your day. If it's all seriousness and suffering even the most disciplined people will eventual tire of it and find another way to live. If it's all spring break then nothing gets done. Finding the right compromise between beneficial suffering and delayed gratification versus happiness and play is the key to longevity in the sport. We take a stance of hard work time but very relaxed playtime afterwards with lots of poking fun at each other and off-limits humor - the best antidote to the biggest problem of long-term development - burnout. Everyone has their own correct balance - somewhere you have to find yours.

If your back is on the floor - then you know that your opponent can't get to your back:
There are several good ways to defend your back but one of the safest and most effective is to work to get your back to the floor. Part of the problem of defending your back is that it's tough to SEE what your opponent is doing - he is behind you after all - you have to feel it. The beauty of getting your back to the floor is that vision is unnecessary - it's simply impossible for an opponent to get behind you if you put the floor on your back first. Like any escape - hit it early - the longer you delay the harder it gets. Bear in mind that ultimate it will lead you back to the safety of guard - so be ready to pull your legs in tight upon completion.

Opening gambits:

Jiu jitsu is a game with a lot of chaos built into it that prevents us from ever fully knowing what will happen or what the best options are - nonetheless when you first go to engage with an opponent there are only so many opening moves. This is one area where you can go into a match with a pretty good idea of what will unfold, based on initial movements. Make sure you have at least a few favorite options to come out with a plan rather than just come out and see what happens. I'm sure many of you will recognize the opening gambit shown here by a Craig Jones - a squad favorite and perfect for anyone looking to get off to a strong start via leg locking.

Getting pinned is bad - getting pinned AND getting your limbs extended out and away from your torso is even worse:

When most people get to a dominant pin they are so happy to score the points that they don't take the next step and seek to isolate a limb by working it out and away from the torso. Never forget that the ultimate aim of grappling (not fighting) is to submit an opponent. A positional pin is a means to that end - only when you take the extra step of limb isolation will you bridge the gap between position and submission. Next time you get to a dominant pin, don't be satisfied with the pin - go further and work the limb away from the torso - you will find immediately that you make the pin stronger and suddenly become far more threatening to your opponent. Best of all you will start submitting a lot more opponents.

Tension and relaxation:

Jiu jitsu is a game that requires from us great variations in states of muscular tension and relaxation. If you're too tense too long you will quickly exhaust yourself and your movements will be stiff and inefficient. Too relaxed too long and you won't be able to hold and control a wildly resisting opponent when pinning him or going for submission attempts. Different scenarios require different physical dispositions in terms of muscular effort. The LESS CONTACT with an opponent the LOWER the tension level. The more you engage in MOVEMENT the LOWER the tension levels. The more you engage in STOPPING movement the HIGHER the tension levels. Use these simple rules to guide your degree of muscular tension so that you can exhibit good endurance and good movement quality while at the same able to lock someone in place with sufficient control to pin opponents and finish them.

Getting out of trouble – and putting the other guy into trouble:

If there is one skill in Jiu jitsu that NEVER goes out of style it would be getting out of bad position. I don't care how talented an athlete is - we all make mistakes and at some time we all find ourselves fighting for survival out of pins. My approach to pin escapes is a little different from most. I train my students to work in two phases. First the escape itself - then to develop a sensitivity to when the danger is past and then AN IMMEDIATE AND AGGRESSIVE COUNTERATTACK THAT FEEDS OFF YOUR OPPONENTS

DESIRE TO REGAIN THE PIN. This takes the humble art of defense into the devastating art of counterattack. Most athletes are satisfied with just getting. I teach to go the extra distance AND FINISH EVERY ESCAPE WITH SUBMISSION COUNTERATTACK WHENEVER POSSIBLE - and in MANY cases it is possible. Take this approach and you'll soon find that your submission percentages double. Tomorrow I will release my NEW WAVE JIU JITSU escapes into counterattacks instructional video and showcase this attacking philosophy into your defense.

The power of escape:
When we think of powerful moves in Jiu jitsu you typically picture a slamming takedown or a bone crunching submission hold, or perhaps an immovable pin or unstoppable pass. We don't typically think of escapes as demonstration of power - but they are - in a different way. Those typical power moves, hard takedowns, crushing submissions etc. are all demonstrations of power over the opponents BODY. Escapes exert their power on an opponent's MIND. Imagine working hard to take an opponent down, pass his hard and get to your favorite finishing position and then have an opponent repeatedly escape. Worse still, every time he escapes he immediately counterattacks and almost catches you as you are forced to flee and start all over again. Hard work is tough, but repeated hard work with no forward progress and no prospect of it finishing is hard for the mind to handle. That's exactly what unstoppable escapes do to an opponent's mind in a match. If you can send a clear message to an opponent that he has no means of controlling and finishing you - the longer that match goes the worse he will begin to feel inside. Every escape brings your confidence up

and his down. In a long match where points are not a consideration this is a huge factor. There is no lonelier feeling than being fatigued and disheartened by repeated frustration of being close to victory but never able to secure in a match that goes until one of you quits and you now know you have no means of making the other guy quit because he can escape all your best positions without a problem. Here Garry Tonon launches into a strong kipping escape out of mount, about to be followed by a devastating heel hook follow up. There is a reason why he attacks so fearlessly and without abandon in his matches - because he fully believes in his ability to get out of any hold should his attack misfire in any way. The power of Escapes is thus not over the body but over your mind and your opponent's mind - now THAT'S real power.

When the pressure is on:
How many moves do you REALLY know? We all think we have a good idea of the size of our skill set. In truth however, the only time you find out is when you play under pressure. ONLY THE MOVES YOU WILL USE WITHOUT HESITATION IN THE BIGGEST MATCH OF YOUR LIFE ARE YOUR TRULY KNOWN BY YOU - everything else can be considered only as moves you are familiar with, but not truly known. Your job is to slowly build upon that small set in two ways. First, refining still further the moves already there. Second, adding a few new ones every year to a level where you would pull the trigger with them without hesitation in a high-pressure match against your toughest rivals with everything on the line. In championship training this is the acid test to see how big your skill set really is.

When you're starting on the path to back control mastery - focus on the upper body first:
The back is the most dominant position in a grappling match without striking. Nothing else creates such a mismatch between the control and submission opportunities of the attacker vs the defender. The SCORE comes from the legs - getting your two legs hooked into an opponent's hips is what creates the score. However, the real-world control comes from maintaining chest to back connection with or without the legs. When you first begin the back game - focus on the upper body connection first and foremost. You can always get the hooks in later to score. Use your arms in seatbelt or double under control to form a tight initial connection and create a strangle threat. As you get more advanced you'll find there are ways you can get legs in first without conventional upper body connection but they aren't the best place to start since you'll be using those far less than conventional methods.

When you're the more experienced or bigger partner - start in bottom position with disadvantage:
We all have a wide variety of training partners. Inevitably there will be big variations in size and skill level among them - so don't treat them all the same. When you are more experienced or bigger - don't start neutral as you would for someone your own size or skill level - start with some form of disadvantage so you get more out of the session and work skills you might not otherwise work and at the same time make it more competitive. When you do this, you can be

in a room full of small white belts and still get a good workout. It's not about who you beat in the gym - it's about beating who you were yesterday - and starting with disadvantage is the best way to do this when training with people you already know you can easily beat.

Countdown in Texas:
The squad is in Austin Texas getting ready for the big WHO'S NUMBER ONE grappling show tomorrow night. Gordon Ryan will take on one the squads biggest rivals, Vagner Rocha. Both athletes have met before but in a lighter weight category and both have changed a lot since their last meeting. Nicky Rod is back on stage. He will take on the great ADCC champion Yuri Simoes. Mr. Simoes is one of only three athletes ever to win ADCC gold in two different weight categories. Both have a high energy takedown focus game and neither likes to give an inch of ground - this one should be a great match! Oliver Taza will take on Johnny Tama in another exciting match up. Today was weigh in with all athletes close to each other in weight to make for a great show tomorrow! Now it's training time and then tomorrow the big show!!

Victory in Texas!!
The squad had a great night here in Austin tonight with three athletes competing and three victories at The Who's Number One grappling show. Gordon Ryan won via submission - a triangle that he selected prior to the match - against the great ADCC medalist and squad rival, Vagner Rocha. Nicky Rod took on the great Yuri Simoes,

the two-time ADCC gold medalist in two weight categories. Nicky Rod showed his incredible Jiu jitsu development by passing repeatedly against a great champion who is almost never scored on in even the highest-level competition. Oliver Taza won a very tightly contested match against outstanding world champion Johnny Tama. Mr. Tama played a strong positional game while Mr. Taza focused most on submission attacks. It was great being back in Texas and great to see the squad athletes showcase the skills they work so hard to perfect in the gym out on the stage. Now it's back to Puerto Rico to get Craig Jones, Nicky Ryan and Ethan Crelinsten ready for big challenges next month!! Hope you all enjoyed the show!!

Starting with a skill set - the example of a Nicky Rod:

A situation I often see as a coach is that of a talented athlete from another sport such as wrestling, Judo or Sambo coming into Jiu jitsu. It's natural to want to use and adapt your skills to the new game. This conversion can be done fairly quickly and easily and usually gets good results. My belief however, is that it will rarely get you GREAT results. You have to go further and learn new skills from the bottom up in your new sport if you really want to become exceptional. A good example is that of Nicky Rod. He was a high school wrestler - he also did a year in D3 college - so he had a solid enough background in wrestling without being anything exceptional. Whenever you're in this situation it's natural to just train in Jiu jitsu so as to exploit this initial skill set that you have. So, wrestlers will often just work submission defense and look to develop a game that lets them win on their primary skill - takedowns. This will win you matches at local level but will never get you to championship level. To do that you have to immerse yourself in the new game you are studying. It's not easy to give up a strength and work on a weakness. It's so much easier just to stay within the safety of your strength. Nicky Rod did a fine job of practicing in new skill areas - guard position, submission holds and guard passing. It showed this weekend when he took on the great Yuri Simoes. Yuri is one of only three people who have won two gold medals in two weight classes in ADCC (Gordon Ryan and Jeff Monson are the other two). Most people thought Nicky Rod's only path to victory was through wrestling takedowns. Even though Yuri is one of the best takedown artists in Jiu jitsu he intelligently sat to guard to deny what most people thought was the only way Nicky Rod could win. What happened next was shocking for many observers. Nicky Rod went immediately on the offense with a pure Jiu jitsu skill - guard passing. In fact, there was almost zero wrestling in this match. It was won with Jiu jitsu skills. It was a fine example of immersion in a new sport winning at high levels - an example many others can learn and profit from.

Don't be satisfied with good when great is right there for the taking:
Getting into a dominant pin is a good thing but if you want to go the extra distance and progress from position to submission, then you must learn to isolate limbs away from the torso to set up submission entries. Don't congratulate yourself when you get to your pin - immediately start the task of isolating an arm and head. It will make it tougher for him to escape and easier for you to finish. The earlier you start the task the better your chances of succeeding. Program

yourself to WORK from the pin rather than REST from the pin, and you will be a finisher faster than you thought possible.

The not-so-gentle art:
Jiu jitsu, like all combat sports, aspires towards maximum efficiency in physical output. It strives to use the least amount of energy to get the job done. This is often misconstrued to mean that everything should appear effortless and flowing in execution. It is certainly true that for the majority of any given match your body ought to be fairly relaxed and loose to allow efficient movement, but there are definitely times when you want to exert near maximal muscular contraction and effort for short bursts. THIS is part of the pathway to true efficiency. If you are too relaxed when applying a submission hold and the opponent escapes - then you have to start all over again - necessitating the repeated expenditure of a large amount of energy and potential risk of losing. There is nothing efficient about that. True efficiency is being relaxed when appropriate (usually the majority of the match) but also tight when appropriate (usually for short bursts when scoring or finishing). This way you don't waste energy getting to a scoring or finishing situation and fail due to lack of tight connection/power and then have to repeat yourself all over again. One quick burst of near maximal energy output that ends a match is not as fatiguing as twenty minutes of relaxed sparring that requires you to keep going and going due to repeatedly failing to score or finish because you were too loose at the critical moment. So yes, stay relaxed most of the time - but when it's time to go – GO.

What opportunities do you see in this moment?

Could act upon them in the time available? In any neutral situation in Jiu jitsu both athletes have opportunities for advancement or even outright victory. The first step is visual/mental. You have to SEE and IDENTIFY an opportunity before it becomes possible for you to go to the next step which is physical/skill based, that is to ACT upon that vision with sufficient prowess to get the job done. Every physical action begins as a recognition in the mind. It's no good recognizing the opportunities but being too slow or unwilling to pull the trigger and take the physical action required to make it happen. Developing both aspects is crucial. Skill without vision will never be utilized. Vision without skill will achieve nothing. Train yourself to see opportunities and act on them and you will be on the way to superior performance.

Priorities:

In any given second by second scenario in Jiu jitsu there is a LOT going on. It's easy to get swamped by all the information coming in and the need for decisions going out. When it all seems too confusing - prioritize the most important things and temporarily ignore the rest. For example, when attacking the back in a scramble there are many things to be concerned about - getting your hooks in to score, sinking the strangle hand to finish, winning the hand fight, tilting your opponent to your preferred side etc. but always the priority should be maintaining CHEST TO BACK CONNECTION. Without that none of the other things are possible SO THAT TAKES PRECEDENCE OVER EVERYTHING ELSE. For any given situation, no matter how confusing, ask yourself what is the single base requirement needed to fulfill all the other desires you have in that scenario - and put all your focus on that until you've got things under control and can start to put your attention elsewhere. Using this simple PRIORITY PRINCIPLE will give you direction and purpose in even the most confusing and complex situations in Jiu jitsu.

Defensive soundness:

I'm sure you've all been to a boxing match and heard fools in the audience randomly screaming "KEEP YOUR HANDS UP!" every twenty seconds regardless of what is actually happening in the ring. Well, underneath it all there is some wisdom. Boxer keep the hands up in order to cover the chin and make it less accessible to a blow. Observation will quickly reveal good boxers don't always keep their hands up, but they do whenever they NEED to. Grapplers too need to protect and cover their chin when they need to - but for different reasons. We don't need to worry about a blow to the chin, but rather a hand/wrist sliding under the chin to set a stranglehold. As such there is a need for us also to keep our hands up as a block when appropriate to catch not punches to the jaw, but strangles UNDER the jaw. Learn to keep your hand up and ready to block - just like a good boxer you don't want your hands always in defensive mode - otherwise it can stifle your offense a little - but when it's needed it BADLY needed - so get those defensive hands up and ready to save you.

In a game where control is everything -

using frames to prevent an opponent from establishing controlling grips and position is a huge part of your development. The centerpiece of your frames will always be the link between your knees and elbows. The closer your opponent gets to you - the closer your knees and elbows need to be together.

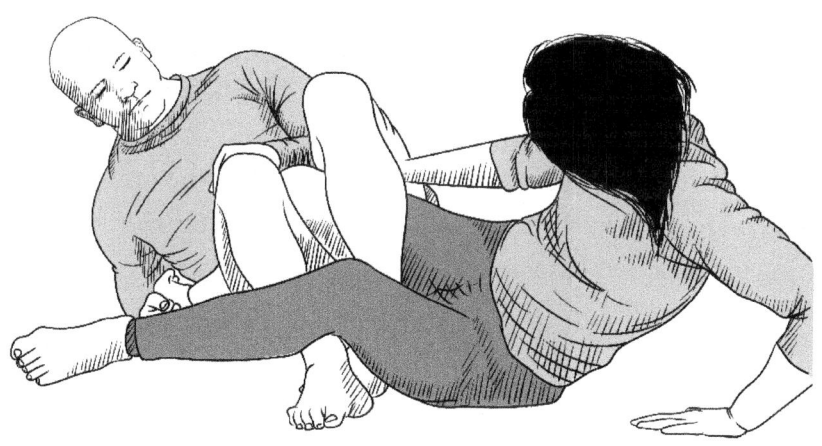

With regards technique –

fashions come and go - what is popular today can be replaced by tomorrow - but underneath that surface technique lies something permanent, something deep and unchanging whose weight will give your game gravitas - the bedrock of the art - PRINCIPLES. Focus on those and your game will never go out of style.

Hands and head:

When you first make contact, with an opponent whether it be standing or from seated guard situations, the first points of contact with your opponent will typically be at the hands and forehead. Learning to place them so as to create defensive barriers and then manipulate them to create offensive opportunities is a big part of your opening gambits in Jiu jitsu. Understand always that your head and hands have both defensive and offensive value - but that in most cases it's tactically smart to take care of your defensive responsibilities before your offensive ones. Your head and hands are both a barrier and a key to your opponent's door that can give you access to everything else. Use them wisely from the start of each engagement and you will stop an opponent in his tracks whilst setting up your own attacks.

Create a strong initial threat and you will own the next move:

If you can put your opponent under extreme pressure with a given move it will elicit such a focus on defense that you will have a considerable tactical advantage in any follow up move. An opponent whose entire attention is bound up defending one move will be very vulnerable to any subsequent move. It is up to you however, to develop the sensitivity to know how to keep the pressure on the first attempt but know inside that it's unlikely to break through the opponent's defense and concoct a good follow up. There are two ways you can fail with this. The first is Tunnel vision that keeps you focused only on that first move when it's becoming clear that it won't work. The second is not putting enough pressure on the first move so the opponent is not sufficiently distracted and can thus defend the second move as soon as you attempt it. Learning to balance these two demands is a big part of your development towards a strong offense.

Stripping away choice:
The essential nature of Jiu jitsu can be explained very easily. At the onset of a match both athletes can move as they please. As a result, they each have many thousands of options as to what they may do. The second they come to grips that number of options drops dramatically as now they have to move in ways that account for the grip and control of their opponent. As one athlete gains increasing dominance in position the number of sensible options for the other athletes diminishes further still. As the positions and grips become still more dominant those available options for the defensive athletes fall down to less than a dozen. By the time a real finishing hold has been achieved the options can be counted on one hand. Your goal is always to reduce the infinite number of available options at the onset of the match to two options that signals the end of the match - submission or the physical consequences of refusal to submit. Starting to see the game as a battle to reduce an opponent's options is a big part of your development. This is the mindset that enables you to see an opponent's future actions - not because you have some superpower to see the future, but simply because you know the limited options he will have available ahead of time.

Air time:
Sweeps in Jiu jitsu all score the same amount regardless of amplitude. Indeed, powerful sweeps often result in reduced control after the sweep and allow an opponent to scramble out to avoid conceding the score. Nonetheless there is something to be said for big sweeps - they have a disorienting effect that can sometimes lead into submission attempts after the sweep. In addition, they create a definite sense of power that will send a message to opponent and create some fear/respect for the next sweep that may create over reactions that you can exploit. So even though most of the time control is more important than amplitude, every so often you can let fly and make an opponent fly the unfriendly skies.

The power of kimura:
Of all the major submission holds, kimura is in my experience the one which creates the most devastating injuries when opponents fight to the end and refuse to tap. All the major submissions are capable of doing serious damage when taken to their conclusion but the extreme rotation power of kimura creates total separation of the joint that often results in gruesome dislocations and on occasion, even spiral fractures of the bones. It is a move that is often disparaged as a strong man's move, but this is an unfair criticism. If you let an opponent lock his hands in front of his torso and fight his two hands with yours - then yes - strength will be the deciding factor. However, if you get an opponent's hand behind his back or use your legs to supply the rotation power against his hands, smaller athletes can definitely use this move against bigger athletes. Understand always that there are many variations of kimura - many of which incorporate the legs and thus avoid the two versus two

hands deadlock and use legs against hands to ensure skill, not strength will be the deciding factor.

Extension:
The essential feature of successful submission attempts is always extension of the limb being attacked away from the torso to a degree that renders it vulnerable. The hardest people to submit are those who contract their limbs in tight to the torso (though by doing so they render themselves vulnerable to other methods of attack). When it's time to lock joints or strangle necks - extension is the ingredient you need. Extended limbs don't stay extended for long in a competitive match - so once you see it - trap it in place.

Don't be afraid to take a step back sometimes:
Jiu jitsu is a game of pressure. As such it's natural to want to always pressure forward and let the other fellow feel the heat. However, this is also a game where sometimes an opponent can get into a sequence of grips that spell danger and you get the feeling that you can't break all those grips before the first attacks will come. In these cases, it can be a good thing to break out of there completely and briefly disengage and then step back into the fray with renewed focus to get a better start. Generally, the athlete who starts better in a given engagement will tend to dominate the rest of that engagement as they have the tactical momentum in their favor. If you feel this is the case - disengage to break the momentum and start again on your terms. Don't be too quick to use this tactic as it can

lead to negative play if overused, but acknowledge that there is a time and place for it when you get off to a bad start and it can definitely save you some grief down the line.

Observation:
The model of development in Jiu jitsu ought always to be as close as possible to the classical model of development in science - of the interaction of hypothesis, experiment and observation and assessment of results in a never-ending rotation that gives provisional but increasingly better answers to the questions you ask. When it comes time to assess the worth of given moves, the merits of your training program, your performance of technique and tactics, nothing beats observation. As an athlete you must keenly observe your performances and make adjustments based in the feedback your eyes give you. Training in itself is the most important thing in the short term, but for long term progress almost as important is observation and assessment of that training that allows you to bring the results of today's workout to tomorrow's workout so that a compounding effect can be attained - only then can you grow over time to the level that you aspire to.

The two greats flaws of ashi garami:
No position has had more radical influence and effect on the no Gi Jiu jitsu game over the last decade than the many variations of ashi garami (a generic term denoting "entangled legs" of which many varieties can be employed). Most of the effect over this time has

come from the leg locking techniques showcased by the squad and those who followed their example. However impressive this development has been to observe, it is important always to consider not just the strengths of every weapon you employ - but also its weaknesses. In the case of the various ashi garami variations the two great weakness are mutual foot exposure and back exposure. Every form of leg entanglement to some degree - some more than others - will expose your feet and your back to an opponent. Usually the less they expose your feet - the more they will expose your back - and the less they expose your back - the more they will expose your feet. As such it is a weapon stands in contrast to the strongest attacking positions of Jiu jitsu such as rear mount - where you can attack with near impunity and focus entirely upon your attack with little to no regard for counter offense. Understanding this must make you circumspect when engaging in offense with ashi garami, and optimistic when engaging in defense - since at any moment you can counter attack very strongly at the feet or back if you play intelligently.

A strange and wonderful thing about this sport
is that no matter how bad a position in which you may find yourself, you are never more than two (or at most three) moves away from victory if you can combine escapes with submissions. Let this insight give you confidence and hope in bad positions and make you circumspect and diligent when in good positions.

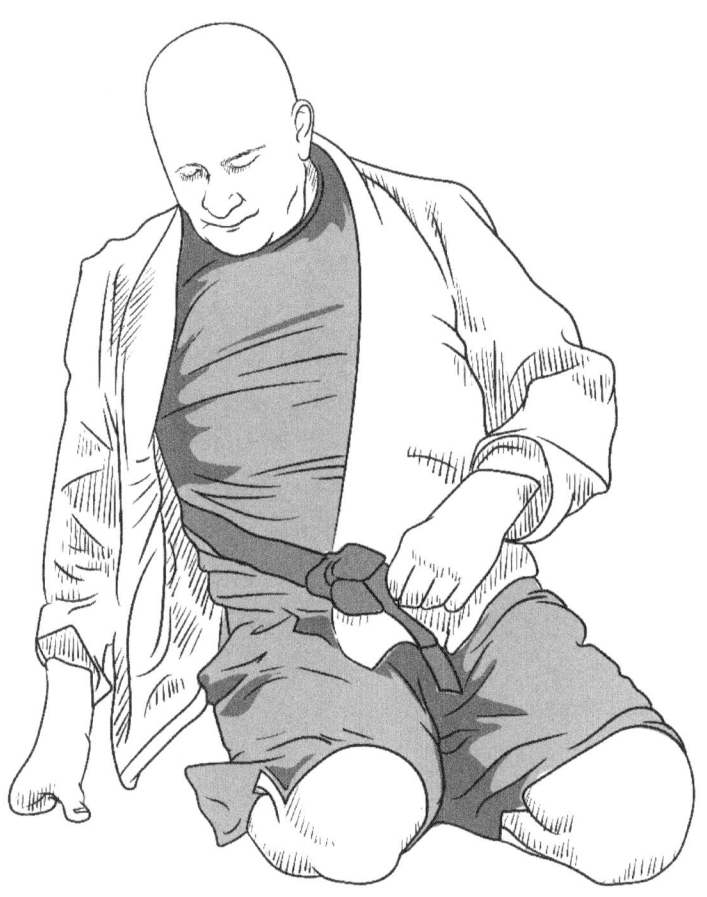

The workout isn't over when your BODY stops moving –

it's over when your MIND stops moving. After every workout there is a time to analyze and recall what you did well, what you did poorly and how you can use those insights to create a better you tomorrow on the mats - use it!

Pace:

The three biggest factors that will determine the outcome of a match will always be technique, tactics and physical/mental attributes. Nonetheless there are other factors going on in a match that play a big role in determining the outcome. One of these is PACE. Every match at a given time has a pace - this can vary throughout a match. Every athlete has a preferred pace - some like it slow, some like it fast. It is very much in your interest to open as close to your preferred pace and as far from your opponents preferred pace as possible. Things get interesting when both of you prefer a similar pace. Then you have to decide whether it's better to stay in your preferred pace (which is also the opponents preferred pace) or take the risk of going out of your comfort zone pace on the understanding that perhaps your opponent will be even more uncomfortable at that pace then you are. If you can play different paces well this can be a big tactical advantage when you come against an opponent who only plays at one pace. In class learn to experiment with pace. Understand that different paces require different physical demands on your part. In your early experiments you will find immediately that you get out of breath more quickly than usual. When you go slower than normal you will often find considerable lactic acid build up and cramps as you clamp down on an opponent with isometric tension to slow him down. Getting used to this different set of physical demands can be tough at first but it can give you considerable tactical advantage to switch pace during a match against an opponent who can't follow the change.

Making strong people weak:
The human body is set up in such a way that it can only exert strength upon objects that are placed in front of it. When we have to exert strength upon objects behind us we simply can't and have to turn ourselves around before we can attempt to do so. When you grapple strong opponents - seek to get behind them. Once you get behind an opponent he simply won't be able to use raw strength against you - he will have to know exactly what to do if he is to get out of the position - strength alone won't be enough. Developing the skills of getting behind opponents is arguably the single best response to the challenge of opponents who feel stronger than yourself. It does better than level the playing field - it slants the field distinctly in your favor regardless of strength disparity. Among the many skills of Jiu jitsu - the skill of slipping behind an opponent at every opportunity is the one most likely to benefit you when going against opponents with a strength advantage over you.

It all starts with push and pull:
once you come to grips with an opponent there will usually be a brief period of push and pull that precedes an attack. This push pull action. Is often overlooked but it is of the greatest importance. In fact, I usually identify the relative expertise level of students by how well that make use of push and pull prior to applying their techniques. The old adage in martial arts is "when pushed, pull, and when pulled, push." There is a lot of wisdom in this. Learning to create reactions and feed off those is critical to your development. You will need to stay relaxed as you play this game within a game and you will need to develop sensitivity to the opponent's reactions to your pushing and pulling. Next time you make grips - start

engaging in push and pull and stay loose enough to read your opponent's reactions and move in response - in time your ability to break through with attacks will increase as a result.

Peeling hands:

Always remember that most grappling techniques begin with grip. The hands and feet are the mechanisms of grip in Jiu jitsu - if you can peel those hands off and deny an opponent his grips it will be very hard for him to initiate grappling techniques. Learning to quickly disarm an opponent by peeling off potentially dangerous grips before they can have effects can save you a lot of trouble down the road. Just make sure you don't focus only upon peeling away grips - you can't play a negative game where you only focus on stopping the other guy doing his work - you have to them assert your own positive attacking grips and get to work yourself. The cycle of grip breaking and grip assertion is what allows good athletes to shut down an opponent's options while asserting their own - a hallmark of good Jiu jitsu.

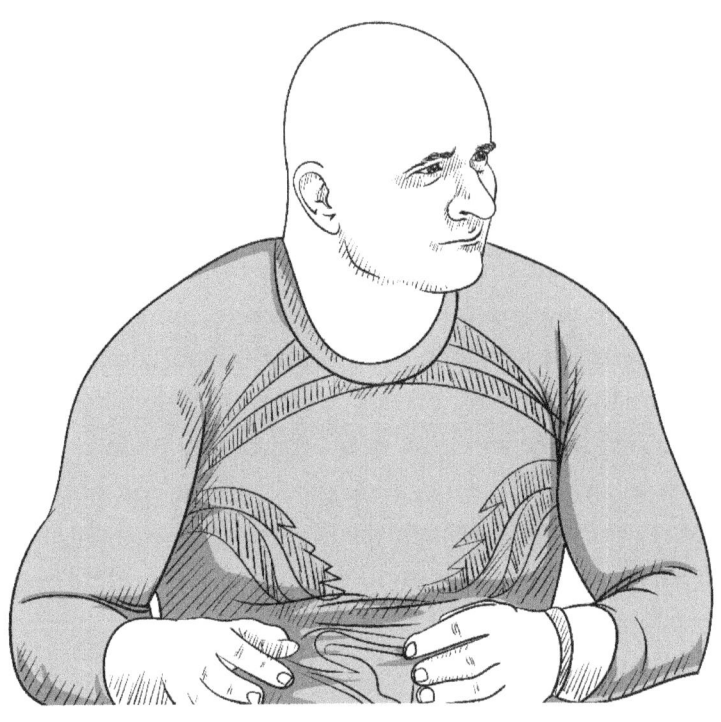

Want to learn to deal with scary situations?
Put yourself there often until it feels like home.

Never forget that training is not about winning - it's about skill development. Don't worry about winning today - worry about building the skills that will enable you to win somewhere out in the future in a match that counts. The gym is the time for innovation and experimentation and development - save your concern for winning and losing for competition.

Defense in depth:
Most of you know that I put an extraordinarily high value on defense training for my students. My belief is that only when students have a strong belief in their defense will they take risks - and any offensive move entails risk - so ironically only athletes who believe in their defense will engage with their offense in high level competition. Understand always that defense comes in different forms based upon how far the opponent has entered into their move. Early defense is the most efficient. The old clock that an ounce of prevention is worth a pound of cure is very true with regards Jiu jitsu. If you can anticipate an attack you will defend it easily. Much more challenging is late defense, where an opponent has performed the move almost to completion and you have to dig your way out. This requires knowledge, skill and a steady nerve. Learn all the aspects of defense from early to late and everything in between - but when you care about winning, be sure to prioritize early defense - it will be easier on your body and less scary for your friends observing on the sidelines!

Every fighter has his favorite weapons –
but keep in mind that the single greatest weapon a fighter can have is the ability to decide an opponent as to his true intentions for the application of all other weapons, including your most cherished will depend in this one.

Submission escapes and fear:
There are two major categories of escape in Jiu jitsu. The first are POSITIONAL escapes - getting out of bad pins such as the mount, side pins, rear mount etc. These are uncomfortable, tiring and generally unpleasant situations but they aren't scary unless they are being done in an MMA context with striking permitted - in standard grappling situations they are unpleasant rather than frightening because pins by themselves don't do any kind of damage. The second category of escapes are SUBMISSION escapes. This is where fear becomes a factor. Submissions can do serious damage if taken to their completion or applied with bad intentions. As such escaping from submission has a mental aspect to it that positional escapes don't - you have to be able to overcome the natural fear of bodily harm and stay focused on the relevant details of getting out. Once the submission is locked on, things happen quickly and you have to make a quick choice between submission and escape. In the gym it's prudent to err on the side of caution. Nonetheless nobody likes to lose by submission and so there is a strong motivation to learn submission escapes. Understand that the further you get into the submission the harder it becomes to extricate yourself. Early detection and avoidance usually get better results than last ditch heroics. But still, it's good to be able to show the skills of Houdini and get out of seemingly hopeless situations and escape. The biggest

factors working against you are TIME, INTENSITY and PANIC. When you start out, make sure you have a partner who can dial back the speed and intensity of his submissions to something pretty mild so that you can think without panic and perform the appropriate escape. Practice light and slow and get a gradual feel for the position and what you can and can't take. Very slowly start increasing the speed and intensity over time. Like any other skill, practice over time can make what was once a very scary situation and make it quite manageable. Note the relaxed demeanor of Nicky Ryan as he methodically works his way out of a potential heel hook situation.

Whatever skill level you are today
will be 70% a reflection of your training behavior over the previous five years and 30% a reflection of the previous three months. Failure to apply yourself well in either category can have serious ramifications for your performance here and now.

Counting down in Austin,
Texas: Nicky Ryan and Ethan Crelinsten will take on exceptionally tough opponents tomorrow night at the WNO Grappling show on Flo Grappling Mr. Ryan will take on the very formidable PJ Barch who combines a D1 Wrestling pedigree with black belt Jiu jitsu to form a very dangerous hybrid game matched with his impressive physicality. Mr. Barch has a been a very tough rival for the squad for a long time with standout performances in the classic EBI shows when the squad began! Ethan Crelinsten will rematch the

brilliant ATOS prodigy Kade Ruotolo who forms one half of the powerful Ruotolo brothers - they have also been powerful adversaries of the squad with wins for both sides. They have a brilliant and dynamic game with tremendous endurance and a cracking pace. Everyone has weighed in successfully and now just light workout tonight and all action tomorrow night! Hope you enjoy the show!

Your game will be made vastly more effective by having one or two truly strong attacks that create defensive over reactions from opponents that set up all your moves.

Danger zones and safe zones:
Any time you pass through dangerous territory you would never stop in an area that appeared even more dangerous than usual, rather, you'd keep moving until you came across an area that appeared less dangerous, only then would you take a break, reorganize and plot your next move. Jiu jitsu is no different. There are some positions relative to your opponent that are just too dangerous to stop and take a break. There are others that are safe enough to take a temporary respite and use some time to make a good next move. How safe these areas really are will vary. Really dominant positions such as rear mount give you great opportunities to really slow things down and consider your options. More often the safety zones are not that safe - they just take away the immediate threat. He has stepped out of a danger zone (directly in front of the legs) to a zone that offers a very temporary safety - he will have to move quickly from here if he is to advance to greater safety and prevent being put right back into the danger zone. Make your early movements when you first engage away from immediate danger zones and work progressively through the various safety zones and you'll be able to focus more on offense and get less distractions from having to fend off your opponent's attacks.

I started my career teaching introductory classes to one or two white belts at a time.
Then I built up to small beginner classes with five or six people. In time I averaged over a hundred people per class in the lunch hour with some of the greatest combat athletes in the world. Now I've come full circle and I'm back to teaching tiny classes. I was able to create a sense of progress and development in all cases regardless of

class size, location or talent level. Your rate of progress towards your goals has much more to do with what is inside your head than where you are, who is around you or how many people there are. Know what you want - acquire the skills to make it possible - formulate a plan to get there - have the discipline to stay the course and the wisdom to modify the plan in the face of changing circumstances and you can shock the world regardless of where you are and who or how many you are surrounded by.

Visitors:
We always love having visitors come by and train - they always provide new perspectives and challenges that help growth in all directions. Today we had the privilege of working with world class wrestlers associated with the Penn State program! Jaime Espinal, Anthony Cassar and Josh Rodriguez they showed how at the end of the day, all grappling styles are related - learning some Jiu jitsu applications of their wrestling skills they had a great workout with the squad! Once we open up our own place with more mat space we look forward to hosting more visitors and growing this sport some more!

One strong threat will create defensive over reactions –
THAT'S the best time to attack! A strong first attack is a wonderful thing - it will get you a lot of wins if you really excel at that attack. The real benefit in the long term won't come from that strong initial attack however - it will come from exploiting the predictable

reactions to that attack with follow up moves you have learned to mate with the initial attack. Ask yourself what your favorite attacks currently are. Then ask yourself what are the most common defensive reactions you encounter in response - and then the big question - what are the logical responses to those reactions? This is the pattern of behavior you want to establish in your game. You don't need a vast array of attacks but you do need some strong ones that create a genuine threat. It is the threat from which the breakthroughs will come. Organize your game into initial attacks and linked follow ups and watch your submission rate improve massively over just strong attacks in isolation.

Threats:
Our behavior is immediately changed whenever we feel a significant threat. It usually puts us into a defensive mindset where we tend to be more concerned with addressing that threat than we are in attacking the opponent. This tells you something important. Whenever you want to shut down an opponent's initiative - put him under some threat that throws him into a reactive/defensive mindset where he is more worried about what you're doing to him than what he wants to do to you. Nowhere is this principle easier to apply than when you are attacking from the back. Sometimes we get so focused on holding the position or trapping an opponent's arms that an opponent feels little threat beyond the position itself. As a result, he can focus on his escapes and take liberties with his head and arm positions to facilitate his escapes. All that changes when you create a powerful threat of strangulation every time his hands

and chin fall even a little out of defensive position. Now he has to focus so much on the strangle threat that escaping the actual position becomes forgotten as he has to focus entire on protecting his neck. There are many ways this can be applied in Jiu jitsu (and indeed - life). Comfortable opponents are difficult opponents - fearful opponents are subdued opponents - the latter are much easier to control than the former. Here Georges St Pierre does a good job of creating a strangle threat to slow down even a master of escape and counter attack like Gordon Ryan use this principle when you feel opponents don't respect your ability to hold a position.

What's more important –

heuristics or details? When it's time to gain knowledge in Jiu jitsu that improves performance there are two main avenues. The first is HEURISTICS. These are general rules of thumb that guide behavior. So, for example, "whenever possible try to pass guard in a direction opposite that which your opponent's knees are pointing" is a general piece of advice that guides guard passing behavior in a wide set of circumstances and generally aids guard passing performance. It is easy to remember and gives good guidance in many situations. The second are technical DETAILS. These are situation specific and often difficult to remember under stress. In truth you need both. HEURISTICS WITHOUT DETAILS ARE INEFFECTIVE AND DETAILS WITHOUT HEURISTICS ARE PARALYZING. Make sure your study and general reflections on Jiu jitsu involve both.

Create a three-month challenge for yourself:
Getting good at Jiu jitsu is mostly about building strong fundamentals and then developing a few favorite moves (the Japanese call them "Tokui-waza") and then a collection of other moves that branch off those favorite moves. That is certainly an excellent approach and that should be where most of your focus goes. Nonetheless I'm sure there are some moves out there that you like but you feel you are simply awful at. I'll give you an example from my life. I was always terrible at knee pick takedowns. I felt good wrestlers use them occasionally on me and they felt really effective but whenever I tried them, I would usually get tossed by uchi mata or lateral drop counters against anyone with good standing skills, so I dropped studying them. In 2003 the Freestyle Wrestling World Championships were held in Madison Square Garden New York City. A dear friend of mine got tickets and after training we walked from Renzo's and went to watch the world's best go head-to-head. It was an amazing event with super star athletes like Buvaisar Saitiev, Yandro Quintana, Cael Sanderson, Daniel Cormier and many others. At one point in the early rounds one athlete hit a beautiful knee pick and I remember thinking - man...I have to try again - it's too good to just ignore. Back at the gym I tried hard to improve my application of it. For three months I tried different methods, entries, sets and finishes. One day I got into a single leg and failed - switched to a knee pick and nailed it!! I never got really strong at it - but I at least got competent at it to a level where I could surprise an opponent with it and score occasionally. Interestingly many years later my students Georges St Pierre and Gordon Ryan were able to use it to win some of their biggest matches - so as a coach learning more about had the double benefit of helping other people to use it successfully even if it was never one of my main moves. I'm sure you have a move like this. One that isn't your strongest but you're interested in it. Try studying it for three

months and see what you can do. Perhaps it can become one of your back up weapons when your big guns aren't working.

When you watch Jiu jitsu:
Every time you watch Jiu jitsu you get a chance to train your mind in the same way that every time you step on the mat you get a chance to work your body. See it for what it is - an opportunity to train. Don't watch passively. Most people just watch to see the outcome. The outcome only affects the players. In order to benefit YOU, you must become a PARTICIPANT not just an OBSERVER. That means putting yourself mentally into the action. You must see yourself as one of the athletes and ask yourself what you would be doing second by second in response to the action unfolding in front of you. Passively watching for the outcome is fun - but improvement will come from actively engaging on a mental level where you become a mental participant. Then watching is transformed from being an enjoyment to a source of progress that you can carry over into your next physical training session.

Dual threats:
Quite often when attacking with submission holds you can create a threat with two submissions at the same time. As an opponent goes to defend one - he falls victim to the other. Usually, one strong submission is more than enough but when the opportunity to attack simultaneously with two arises - you are wise to take it. Think about a triangle attack - whenever you have it you almost always have a

simultaneous opportunity to attack with juji gatame armbar, kimura or wrist lock. Every submission hold can be used in SEQUENCE as part of a combination attack - but only a select few can be attacked SIMULTANEOUSLY. Make sure you know them - even though are relatively rare, they can be an extremely valuable addition to your submission arsenal.

Getting out of a bad situation is good –
but much is getting out of a bad situation and IMMEDIATELY COUNTER ATTACKING so that you seize the initiative of the match again. For every escape there is always a critical point where you have broken away - THAT is the point where your mind should switch from defense to offense and change your action from escape to attack. Don't be satisfied with getting out - aim higher and look for counter attacks the moment you pass the threshold of escape.

Pins are a means not an end:
A very distinctive feature of my students' approach to Jiu jitsu is to never be happy with an upper body pin. We get taught to value guard passing and pinning so much - indeed, the point system rewards you and enables you to win matches with pins alone - that it's easy to skip over the extra step of finishing from a pin. Good Jiu jitsu always sees a pin as a means to the end of submission holds. That means you must go behind the act of pinning chest to chest and into the more difficult world of LIMB ISOLATION AND CONTROL. Only an isolated limb can be submitted. Learning to

draw a limb away from the torso and into a finishing hold can be a frustrating experience. Limbs by their very nature are more difficult and intricate to control than torsos and now you need to explore the more complex world of levers and fulcrums. You must push yourself past pins and into submissions if you are to satisfy the ideal of Jiu jitsu.

We all like to win –
but if you don't make training fun and enjoyable, you won't last long enough to build winning skills.

What's your mindset here?
You're under attack. A stud opponent has your leg in a vulnerable position and is working intelligently and swiftly towards a finish. How is your mind reacting? The lowest level of reaction is PANIC. The second level of reaction is to scramble into intelligently directed defense and ESCAPE. The third and highest level of reaction is to see the possible of COUNTERATTACK even as you navigate into an escape. TO SEE THE POSSIBILITY OF DEVASTATING COUNTER OFFENSE WHEN EVERYONE ELSE SEES ONLY DEFENSE IS THE MARK OF A SUPERIOR SUBMISSION EXPERT. Train your mind to think this way and you will distinguish yourself from the crowd.

It's damn hard to hide your legs from someone who is actively looking for them:

One of the most obvious features of the leg lock revolution in Jiu jitsu was the prevalence of leg locking from bottom position rather than the more favored top position of earlier generations. When I began Jiu jitsu leg locking was usually seen as an alternative to passing guard from top position - if you couldn't pass - you tried some leg locks instead. This opened leg locks to the old criticism that if they failed you lost top position. Over time I came to believe that in fact the most profitable entries into leg locks were generally from bottom position where they could be easily combined with a traditional positional sweeping game and take advantage of opponents basing their legs out wide to avoid sweeps and making themselves easy marks for leg attacks. When my students began winning many matches with this method many assumed the reason I favored leg lock attacks as the foundation of our guard attacks is that most opponents of that era did not know much about defending leg locks. This is incorrect. Even when my students spar against each other and know that their opponents have excellent leg lock defense, I STILL advocate using leg locks as the basis of their guard game. Why? BECAUSE THE LEGS ARE IMPOSSIBLE TO HIDE FROM AN OPPONENT WHO KNOWS HOW TO ATTACK THEM. Even if the leg locks are well defended by a knowledgeable opponent, THEY PUT THE OPPONENT IN A REACTIVE MINDSET WHERE HE IS MORE CONCERNED WITH DEFENDING HIS LEGS THAN PASSING YOUR GUARD - and once you get them in a reactive mindset you will dominate the direction of the ensuing action. THAT was the tactical reasoning behind making leg lock attacks the centerpiece of our guard game. There is no stance an opponent can take that will hide his legs from attack - it doesn't matter whether he is standing, staggered or square, on one knee, kneeling, squatting, feet inside or feet outside

- whatever - there is always a path to SOME variation of ashi garami and the resulting attacks. This even in a room full of leg lock experts it still makes sense to make leg locks a foundation of your guard game.

If I asked you what your best grappling attack was, I'm sure you could answer in a second –
but if I asked you what your best grappling attack will be next year could you answer so quickly? Don't just focus on where you are now - think ahead to where you want to be in the future.

The rising star of grappling shows Who's Number One run by Flo Grappling in Austin, Texas is on May 28!
Australian superstar Craig Jones will replace Gordon Ryan in the main event. Sadly, Gordon's long battle with a protracted stomach illness is not going well and he will have to step out of the competition circuit until it is satisfactorily resolved. Craig Jones stepped in on short notice to replace him. He has a very tough and dangerous opponent - the great world champion Luiz Panza - a master of leg locks who also excels at upper body submissions and has a great positional game as well. This will be a fascinating contrast in leg locking style. Mr. Panza has devastating Achilles locks with a more traditional Jiu jitsu style - both straight and cross. Mr. Jones has a more modern style focused around twisting locks and a systematic control game based around multiple ashi garami variations. One thing is certain - if either one gets a decisive grip on the leg - it's over! Squad juniors Nicky Ryan and Oliver Taza take on

very impressive opponent. Mr. Ryan will face black belt standout Gabriel Almeida, who has world class Jiu jitsu and also excellent wrestling skills along with a big size advantage over Mr. Ryan. Mr. Taza will take on the brilliant AOJ athlete Johnatha Alves. Mr. Alves has a very polished and refined game with beautiful positional transitions. There are many other great matches on the card, including brilliant American world champion Michael Musumeci! Two of the toughest grapplers in the game, Vagner Rocha of Fight Sports and Josh Hinger of ATOS will clash in what will be a very hard-fought match. Mr. Hinger has an exceptionally dangerous guillotine but Mr. Rocha has proven extremely resistant to even the best submission hunters and has an incredible ability to endure attacks, wear an opponent down get to victory - this should be a really great match. Talented AOJ athlete Jessa Khan takes on Pati Fontes. Both of these stand out athletes are really committing to the no Gi game and this match will help them on their path to the top of the women's division. I think Mica Galvao vs Andrew Tackett may be the match to watch! Hope you all enjoy the show!

Never forget

that ninety percent of the outcome of a bout is determined before the athletes even step on to the mat. Focus most of your energy on PREPARATION rather than the bout itself and the results you seek will generally follow as naturally as night follows day.

I'm excited to have another chat with one of my favorite people in martial arts –

Joe Rogan - on his podcast show tomorrow afternoon here in Austin, Texas. Mr. Rogan has done an incredible job over the years of highlighting the role of Jiu jitsu in MMA to the biggest audiences in the world. He has a been a major factor in the growth of our beloved sport since its earliest days. His show covers every aspect of modern life but our discussion will of course mostly be about Jiu jitsu related themes. Looking forward catching up on Joe Rogan.

Focus is everything in this game.

Mentally, focus yourself on the next step on the chain to victory - physically, focus a greater percentage of your strength upon a lesser percentage of an opponent's strength at a vulnerable point of his body and you will break him.

Victory in Texas!!

The squad came out strong tonight in Austin, Texas at the WHO'S NUMBER ONE grappling show tonight - four athletes competed with four decisive victories! Australian grappling super star Craig Jones showed his stellar development with a near perfect submission victory over great Jiu jitsu world champion Luiz Panza at the very start of his match with a beautifully applied heel hook. Mr. Jones has deeply impressed all of us with his progress over the last three years and he showed it publicly here tonight with a flawless victory. Nicky Ryan showed his rapidly developing takedown and passing skills with multiple takedowns and passes to rear mount against the formidable world champion Gabriel Almeida despite the considerable size difference. Oliver Taza took on the brilliant AOJ athlete Johnatha Alves and was able to pass and briefly hold mount and then go into several powerful heel hook attacks. Mr. Alves showed great courage to hold out despite the pain but Mr. Taza took a decisive victory. Demian Anderson took on 10th Planet standout Luis Quinones. He weathered an early storm with impressive calm for a developing athlete and came back to win by a beautiful stranglehold after some nice positional control. Thanks as always to Garry Tonon and Gordon Ryan for help preparing and coaching the squad for action. Now it's back to Boston to film another instructional video and then to Puerto Rico to get everyone ready for the next challenge. Thank you to Joe Rogan for a great podcast chat! Hope you all enjoyed the show!! Good night from Texas!!

Kuzushi:
Most Jiu jitsu student know that the act of off balancing an opponent is referred to as "kuzushi" in Japanese. Most also realize the importance of this to set up techniques on the feet and also from bottom position on the ground. That's all fine as a theory - but what about practice? How do you know you've done a good job of off balancing an opponent in the heat of sparring or competition to a degree that it will be useful for your move? When working from bottom guard position the single clearest sign is simple - DID YOU MAKE YOUR OPPONENTS HAND TOUCH THE MAT? If the answer is yes - well done - he is definitely out of balance and you are ready to attack. When working your kuzushi on your opponent just

try to involuntarily touch his hand to the mat and then immediately attack. Learn to do it and learn to recognize it as an important sign and your effectiveness from guard will greatly increase.

Bottom game is more difficult for most students to learn than top game:

When I teach people beginning Jiu jitsu I almost always start them with bottom game first. The first skill they must master is pin escapes, since in their early days they will be fighting out of bad positions for most of their training time. Once they learn to escape to guard from a bad pin, they will need to learn to hold on to their guard so that they don't get out but then immediately put right back into the pin they just escaped from - so guard retention is the next skill they need to learn. Then they need to learn to fight effectively from their back as they can now get to and hold a guard - now it's time to attack from there. You can see all these first skills involve fighting from your back. Part of the reason this should be taught first is practical - because as a beginner with no takedown or pinning skills you will almost certainly find yourself underneath opponents. In addition, it recognizes that if you are matched against bigger opponents, you must be able to survive and fight from underneath. The other big reason is that most people find the act of learning to fight from their back more difficult than from on top. Nothing in life prepares you for the movements and techniques of bottom game. I've seen plenty of athletic beginners come in and do pretty well in top position on day one - but never seen that from bottom position. Instinct and natural talent doesn't help much from bottom - you have to learn everything. As such the learning process is usually longer in bottom position than top for most people - SO START

WITH A HEAVIER EMPHASIS ON BOTTOM GAME FIRST - it will give you more development time. You can always play catch up with top skills later.

Breaking rules:

There are many general rules that we usually observe in Jiu jitsu "don't turn away from an opponent," is a common one you hear. Understand always that general rules are usually ABBREVIATIONS of important information - it has to be this way because they are designed to hold as much information in the fewest words. As such, they have exceptions built into them once a little more wordage and information is added. In the case of "don't turn away from an opponent" what is really being expressed here is "don't turn away from an opponent in ways that expose your back." Once you realize there are ways to turn away from an opponent that DON'T expose your back, then you will immediately see it's ok to turn away provided you take some precautions. The general heuristic rules are of immense value because they pack a lot of information into short, easily remembered packages - but realize that every simplification has its limits and exceptions - sometimes those exceptions can be of great value to your performance!

Athlete safety in training:

As a coach one thing I take very seriously is athlete safety in training. The single most common reason for derailed training programs is serious injury. We are all mature enough to realize that a combat sport that focuses primarily upon breaking limbs and strangling people carries a risk of injury. We also accept that as long as the risk is inside acceptable parameters the benefits of Jiu jitsu skills are absolutely worth whatever the risks of injury are. My question as a coach is always to ask how to keep those parameters acceptable. This week I filmed in conjunction with BJJ Fanatics a video on training safety and how to reduce the risk of severe or catastrophic injury in Jiu jitsu. Periodic minor injuries are all part of the fun of the game - we all accept that - but no one wants to go to hospital or worse, send a friend to the hospital with an injury that was entirely avoidable. I am going to release this video for free as a guide to avoiding unnecessary injury that I have observed over the years and which made a concrete difference in my training room. A few simple training protocols can really make a difference. Pareto's principle applies in so many aspects of life - including Jiu jitsu injuries. A few moves cause the overwhelming majority of severe/catastrophic injuries and removing them and replacing them with safer and more effective alternatives makes a real difference in gym safety. I will announce when editing is done and it is released. We all love training and we all accept that accidents happen - BUT UNNECESSARY ACCIDENTS DON'T HAVE TO HAPPEN - to keep your progress strong you need to be in the gym - and severe injuries will keep you out of the gym - so let's train hard but also train SAFE to maximize your progress!!

So often our natural inclination is to turn and run from danger - but in Jiu Jitsu it is very often the case that you do better by moving in towards danger and seek to nullify it rather than fleeing into an even worse predicament.

New talent:
Most people measure the worth of a training program on the basis of the best people in the room. I prefer to assess it on the time it takes new people in the room to make progress towards the level expressed by the best people in the room. Nick Ortiz is a very talented Puerto Rican grappler who has been working with us in NYC and now in Puerto Rico. Last weekend he competed in a local show in Boston after helping me film a new instructional video there. Look at the relaxed poise of his leg lock game as he expresses the fundamental squad leg lock themes of targeting both legs, switching from form of ashi garami leg control to another to compensate for an opponent's defensive movement (switching from one leg to another, from front side to backside back to front side finish and from inside foot position to outside to counter an opponent's defensive turn), culminating in a fine 50/50 finish on the inside shoulder. Well done Nick Ortiz!

It's good to chase after perfection with all your moves – that will greatly benefit your long-term progress - but don't let your current lack of perfection hold you back. Remember that with the execution of any move you don't need perfection to succeed - you only need to execute it better than the athlete in front of you can defend it.

Submission holds and failure:
Submission requires total focus of bodily energy for a long enough time to make an opponent submit (or if he chooses not submit, to experience the consequences of his choice). That can be a very considerable energy expenditure in a short time. If it works - it was definitely worth it. In many cases however, you will see an athlete try as hard as he can, even for extended periods of time, and fail. This can have devastating effects. Physically it can be exhausting to apply maximum isometric tension for too long. It's tough to recover from physical exhaustion at the best of time - in the midst of a highly competitive match is even harder. Psychologically it can severely dent your confidence to try submissions again later in the match and make you second guess yourself every time an opportunity arises. As such, it is extremely important that you develop an internal feeling of what a well applied submission feels like so that you know ahead of time whether it will be worth committing all your reserves into the attempt. With all your favorite submissions try to build this self-knowledge so that next time you are in the position you will know with great confidence that you can give it your all for the time required and make it all worthwhile.

When on top, your first responsibility is balance:
It seems there is always a thousand things going on second by second in Jiu jitsu. It's natural to focus on one or two things and get caught out by ignoring a third or fourth. Sometimes it's good to ignore all the clutter and just focus on most important thing in that position. When it comes to passing guard from top there are a vast number of things that could occupy your attention. You have to avoid getting swept. You have to stay out of submissions. You have to employ some form of guard passing method to improve your position. As your opponent works hard to impose his game from bottom, you can get overwhelmed with all the moment to moment demands of the situation. Understand however that there is one demand that needs to satisfied before all the others - you have to STAY OF TOP. The moment you lose top position you're down on points and you can forget all the passes you were considering a moment ago - you will have to swap over entire now to bottom game. Whenever you feel you have too many competing demands while playing top passing - just focus on retaining top position as your opponent goes for his best sweeps and submissions. The longer you hold top against his attacks the more tired he will become and the easier the secondary task of passing will become.

Triangles –
Making two good choices into one great choice: Among the submission holds in Jiu jitsu there is a basic choice between strangles and joint locks - both are great options. In the vast majority of cases, it's an either/or choice; the triangle however, is one of the few options that allows you to attack both at the same time. It is a superb strangle in its own right, match the impressive power of your legs

against an opponent's neck. However, it also traps, isolates and immobilizes the opponent's arm in ways that allow for easy juji gatame armbar attacks, ude gatame arm bar attacks (reverse arm bar), kimura attacks and wrist locks. Defending one of these is not easy. Defending two at the same time of far harder. Defending two at the same used in combination with the others is damn near impossible. Take advantage of the unique properties of the triangle to improve your submission percentages next time you're on the mats!

If you've got a mat –

you've got a dojo: I've travelled the world and seen every kind of gym from the plushest to the most primitive, in the wealthiest countries and the poorest. I've seen that the gym doesn't matter. The only thing that matters is you and the people around you. If you have passion, knowledge and a plan to transform that knowledge into skill, along with the discipline to stay with that plan and the wisdom to modify it when necessary - you can achieve remarkable things. People count - places don't. Your path to your potential is in you and the people around you, not the building you're in.

Position AND submission?

Usually, we think of positional skills as distinct from submission skills in Jiu jitsu - position comes BEFORE submission after all. However, many of the main submissions blend positional pins with submission. The Japanese are often very wise in the naming of their moves. Their term for the most common form of arm bar is juji gatame. "Juji" means "cross" since the two athletes are generally perpendicular to each other; and importantly "gatame" has a dual meaning of "pin" and "lock." The idea is that the arm bar has the properties of both a pin AND a submission - that the two cannot be separated. You can immobilize someone with an arm bar as you do with a side of mounted pin; only you use biomechanics like advantage through your legs pinning his head rather than body weight. When you practice your submissions, especially the juji gatame arm bar, really focus on the idea of restraining and pinning an opponent first rather than rushing to the joint lock - you will find that emphasizing the dual nature of submission holds makes them far more effective against tough opponents.

It all begins with push and pull:
Open guard is perhaps the most quintessential modern Jiu jitsu position. It probably offers a wider array of potential attacks than any other position in the sport - but they all begin the same way - get a grip and engage in push and pull to break an opponent's stance/balance and create a reaction. If you can reliably initiate the push/pull sequence at the onset of most engagements you will have the foundation of a great open guard. Next time you practice open guard focus first on the preliminary push and pull and your will find that as you improve in this regard, all the other moves you wanted to perform come easier.

Craig Jones and Oliver Taza getting ready for their big matches tomorrow night in Austin Texas:

Another big show in Austin tomorrow for Who's Number One and FloGrappling Craig Jones will take on the extraordinarily talented Tye Ruotolo one of the very best from the outstanding ATOS team. This will be a classic matchup of ATOS athletic movement and physical conditioning against the slower more control-based squad style. Oliver Taza will take on the brilliant Brazilian prodigy Mica Galvao. Mr. Galvao shares a common factor with Mr. Ruotolo - he was literally born into Jiu jitsu. Both have practiced at extremely high level since childhood and so bring a level of knowledge and skill to the game far beyond their years. Amazing work again by the promotion to bring such talented athletes out the stage! Craig and Oliver have trained hard as always but they will be very severely tested by such tough and talented opponents! Keep your eyes on this show tomorrow night!

Victory in Austen!!

Craig Jones had a fantastic back and forth match tonight with the exceptionally talented Tye Ruotolo at WNO Grappling event tonight here in Austin. Mr. Jones was able to show a whole new side to his game that he has been developing with a very fine display of takedowns, takedowns into leg locks, guard passing, submission defense and top pressure to take a unanimous decision over a very game Mr. Ruotolo who never gave up and fought well until the end. It was great to see Craig Jones use the aspects of his game that he uses daily in the gym but has not used in matches. Oliver Taza also competed tonight against the young phenom Mica Galvao. It was a tough physical match and Mr. Galvao showed his developing brilliance to win a strong decision - he will be a great force in Jiu jitsu in the future. Hope you all enjoyed the show! Now it's back to Puerto Rico to get ready for the next big challenge! Wishing you all the best from Austin!!

One of the great honors of my coaching career
was to be involved with the two best ever in their respective arts - Georges St Pierre in MMA and Gordon Ryan in grappling. Watching these two incredible athletes get to the top from quiet and unknown beginnings to be the best of the best was truly an honor. It was amazing them work together on the mat today and learn from each other about technique and tactics in ways that cross over between their respective sports. Jiu jitsu and MMA have always had a close relationship. I still believe that the fundamental appeal of Jiu jitsu is tied directly to fighting, even though they sometimes seem very far apart in some aspects of Jiu jitsu competition. The closer we keep them the healthier for the long-term direction of Jiu jitsu. Congratulations to both men for the incredible success they've had in their respective disciplines, thank you for the inspiration you have generated and the lessons you have shown; and wonderful to see them both in action again on the mats!

Running Georges and Gordon through their guard retention/counter offense drills:
Remember this always - there are ten thousand possible skills from guard - all of them can be effective in their own way - BUT NONE

OF THEM WILL BE EFFECTIVE IF YOU CANNOT EXHIBIT THE FIRST AND MOST IMPORTANT SKILL OF ALL GUARD PLAY - THE ABILITY TO HOLD/RETAIN GUARD LONG ENOUGH TO BE EFFECTIVE. Make retention your first skill in building your guard game and you will create a firm foundation upon which you can build the kind of devastating attacking guard game you see my students employ and which you can learn. Guard retention may not be the most exciting guard skill to learn, but it's the most important because it's the one that all the other skills of guard play depend upon.

Most of the work in Jiu jitsu is done on the floor.
The highest scores and submissions are almost always attained on the mat. Nonetheless standing grappling is a truly vital part of the game, particularly when you explore the relationship between sport Jiu jitsu and fighting. Jiu jitsu has always historically had what I call a "bolt on" approach towards standing skills - they simply ask you to study wrestling (no Gi) or judo (Gi) and bolt those skills on to your Jiu jitsu skills. That can definitely work, but understand that the unique rule set of Jiu jitsu offers many possibilities and opportunities to score and win that go outside of those sports. I believe that long term, Jiu jitsu must develop its own standing game appropriate for its own rule set, which allows the athletes to scrimmage for points and submissions that are quite unique and very interesting and develop a new set of skills in the fascinating grey zone between standing and ground where scramble and scrimmage for the points and positions of the unique Jiu jitsu rule set is the order of the day.

Over budget:

It seems every time we go buy something or invest in some project, the initial price you were given is replaced by a new higher price that leaves you more financially stretched out than you had planned on. Submissions are similar. Whenever you go for a submission hold you will need to control the entire limb that you are attacking. Your opponent will be trying to extract that limb from your control. As a result, there will often be cases where your initial clamp on the limb proves seemed adequate for the task, but as your opponent began to resist it proved insufficient and your opponent escaped. My advice is simple - always over budget with limb control. If you are attempting an arm bar - exaggerate the connection of your hips all the way up to the shoulder. If you're attempting a heel hook, exaggerate your connection all the way up to the opponent's hip. This way when the inevitable resistance comes you will have so much of the limb under your control extrication in the time available will be very difficult indeed. If you need a minimum ashi garami connection fifteen centimeters (half a foot) above the knee to be effective, aim for more than thirty centimeters (one foot), on the assumption that your opponent's resistance will strip away much of that and leave you with the minimum. If you had settled for the minimum connection length as a starting goal you would have failed after resistance had been factored in. Factor in the effects of expected resistance from the onset and you will do much better in tough matches. Here I focus on an ashi garami connection all the way up at the hip in case an opponent goes to slip his leg free - this will give me a surplus of connection that will reduce the effect of resistance.

At the end of the day none of us are special.
Most of our best achievements in life come from doing the little things well for extended periods of time. Stay grounded in the belief that above all, the ACQUISITION OF SKILLS is the single most reliable avenue to human greatness; and acknowledge that whatever achievements you have so far can be quickly eroded by straying away from this fact. Stay grounded with the little things every day and know that observance of these over time will prepare you for the big things that fate will occasionally place before you and for which you will be remembered.

Increasing strength, endurance, tenacity and all the other attributes
of your body and mind will lead to small performance increases that will increase your chance of success at the highest level; but be aware that whatever performance increases you get from improvement in that direction is minuscule compared with the performance increases of five, six, seven or eightfold that you can derive from increases in technical and tactical nuance. Your triangle for example, can be improved a little by making your legs stronger; but it can be improved massively (and immediately) by shifting your leg positioning by just a few inches - This is where the core of performance increases will always come from.

My first two goals when I teach open guard:
Open guard is among the most difficult skills to learn in Jiu jitsu. Part of the problem is that it's a big, interconnected skill area. If you lack skills in one area the whole project can look and feel weak. Another problem is that as you are trying to enact your guard play, your opponent is trying to enact his guard passing. As a result, you have to try to impose your moves whilst simultaneously defending his. This often tends to shut developing students down as they get caught somewhere between their desire for offense and their need for defense. I found over the years most students (above blue belt level - beginners should focus on guard retention first and fundamental sweeps initially) do best when they learn the skills of GUARD RETENTION and LEG LOCKING as their first skills to focus upon. All the other skills of guard play are contingent upon being able to hold a guard for extended periods of time against strong passing pressure. Without that as a foundation I can't show you anything of value from guard. However, you can't just get stuck in defensive cycles where you just defend and defend and defend - you have to carry the attack to your opponent. Learning to tie guard retention into counterattacks is a crucial part of your journey into advanced Jiu jitsu. The most readily available for of attack from guard is leg locking. The legs are almost impossible for an opponent to completely hide from you as he engages in passing. As such, I put a very heavy emphasis on guard retention and leg locking as the basis of my guard play coaching program once students have gone beyond beginner level. Learning to synthesize them leads to a powerful amalgamation of DEFENSIVE RESPONSIBILITY with CONTINUOUS OFFENSE - which is the ideal of good guard play.

When you get an opponent off balance he will be open for attack.

When you get a GOOD opponent off balance, he will throw up his defenses and you will need a second attack feeding off those defenses to break through. When you take a GREAT opponent off balance he will be looking to counter attack the second after he throws up his defenses and you will need to anticipate the few counter attacking options he has from that recovery scenario and base your follow up attacks on that prior knowledge. Your BODY STARTS the attack sequence, but it's your MIND that KEEPS you ahead against the best.

There are many ways to win in Jiu jitsu,

but the single most high percentage, safest, most effective across weight classes, best against bigger/stronger opponents, Gi or no Gi, grappling or fighting - is to get behind them and strangle them - end of story.

There aren't many moves that you HAVE to know –

but a good Guillotine is probably one of them: Jiu jitsu gives you a lot freedom of choice when it comes to move selection. There is a huge variation among the great champions as to what their main moves where. As you get more fundamental the moves become less optional - it's hard to imagine a world champion who had no elbow escape for example. Among the submission holds I always encourage my students to develop a strong Guillotine attack. There are few submissions that are as readily available in all aspects of play without a Gi than the guillotine. Top or bottom, standing or ground, set position or scramble - it's pretty much always available at some point after just a few minutes of action. There are many variations - I favor high wrist variations above all others, but great champions have used many variations with great success so find whichever one works best for you. Because you can easily switch sides with your opponent's head you only need to be strong on one side with the guillotine. In my case I have a good arm in guillotine on my left and a good high wrist on my right - so I can play both sides, but with different variations; but at a minimum have a really strong variation on one side and you will be ready to go!

All alone in a crowded room:
most of our Jiu jitsu lives are lives in a community of friends and teammates, coaches and mentors. You can have great support behind you to help in preparation, but at the end of the day - you walk out on the mat alone. In your own time, focus on building the inner confidence to let all the work you did with your friends in preparation shine when you're out there all alone. Managing the separation of communal training with the aloneness of competition is a big part of dealing with your toughest matches.

It's Fourth of July –
put some fireworks in your Jiu jitsu! It's good to have a Jiu jitsu that has different speeds and approaches so that you can tailor them to

different opponents and game plans. Sometimes a slow, controlling game works best, sometimes a fast-dynamic game is what's needed. The problem however, is that some athletes by their very nature are not fast - so how do they increase the pace of the match? Understand that there are different ways to appear fast than just movement. Consider for example the fact that almost every Jiu jitsu match has numerous stoppages in the action when athletes go out of bounds, have to tie their belt, adjust their uniform etc. Every time this occurs you have an opportunity hustle back to starting position faster than your opponent and increase the pace of the match without being faster during the actual match running time. You can be the slowest guy in the whole competition and still be the first back to the start position every time there is a break in the action. This sends a clear message to your opponent - you might outpace me when the match is on but I'll out hustle you every other time - just as in life - hustle will outlast speed. As a fast opponent tires and looks to take a longer break every time the action stops, he looks and sees you hustle to center mat and you keep the pace as high as you can between the action sequences, he will start to fade both mentally and physically. Remember, are different ways to be fast - if you're slow - find one that works for you. Happy Fourth of July!

Even when in defense -
train your mind to look for counter offense. If your mind is preoccupied only defending a move you make yourself an annoyance to an opponent - but to excel you must go beyond being an annoyance and become a THREAT - that means carrying the spirit of offense within you at all times - even in defense. When the mind is trained to look, it will see. Seeing offense on a defenseless

opponent is easy, but seeing it even on tough, aggressive and attacking opponents is the ideal you must strive for.

Leg entanglements allow you to stay a step ahead at all times in guard play:
An opponent can hide his upper body from submissions quite well no Gi simply by standing up. He can negate whole categories of sweeps by switching between standing and kneeling postures. One thing he can never hide by completely by changing stance is his legs - there is always a way to enter. Once you start threatening the legs your opponent cannot simply ignore it - he has to react. As such you immediately put him in a framework where he is reacting to YOUR game rather than you to his. In combat sports this is a crucial advantage. Learning to dictate the pace and get an opponent into a reactive mindset is a crucial part of guard play - learning to attack legs from everywhere is a great way to do it!

Priorities:
It's a common thing to see a young student attacking enthusiastically from the back and focus too much on the submission rather than positional maintenance. If the attack fails, they also lose the position as well as the submission. Remember, as long has you hold the position, you can fail repeatedly and keep trying and again and again until you get the breakthrough. As such, prioritize the position over any given submission attempt. SUBMISSION FAILURE IS ACCEPTABLE IF YOU MAINTAIN

POSITIONAL INTEGRITY, BUT IF YOU LOSE POSITION YOU LOSE EVERYTHING. When you go for your submissions from the back, monitor your positional robustness at all times. If you ever feel that being compromised - STOP - and recover positional integrity. As long as you do this you can always go back to try again with your submissions

Head control:

There is a reason why they classify us as vertebrates - our spines are the center of our body. On top of that spine is our head. The spine is the longest lever in the human body. The head is at the end of that lever. If you control the head, you can exert tremendous leverage that can be used to control the whole body. Look for opportunities to control the head - many are pretty obvious but some are more subtle. Understand that you can exert pressure on the head in both linear (e.g. snap down) and circular (e.g. crossface) directions - be sure to use both. Understanding Jiu jitsu is to a large degree, understanding the human body and its essential nature. Our spines largely define our physical lives - make sure your Jiu jitsu reflects this fundamental fact.

Your body will be a big part of what determines your game:

Three things determine what your grappling game will be. Your body type, your personality and your coaching lineage. Over the years your game will reflect the average of these three influences.

There is no question that your body type is a very important part of your development. No one knows you better than you do, yet surprisingly I often see students try to take on a game that is poorly suited to their physical body. I am always rather reluctant to tell someone not to partake of a certain game because of their body type - history has shown more than a few examples of athletes who defied conventional wisdom and developed a strong game that did not appear to suit their body. I've seen some short-legged athletes with great triangles. I've seen a few tall athletes who were very good at level changing down to quick and snappy double legs. Nonetheless, experience will guide you in certain directions over time. You will find certain moves come more easily to you than others. Be alert to this! Your own body is talking to you - make sure you listen!

The majority of every match
will be spent in neutral positions where neither of you has an advantage over the other. This is where most of the really hard physical work is done. It easy to get frustrated by the amount of work required to make even small advances, but have faith that every small advance accumulates as pressure over time that will pay dividends further into the match and turn those neutral positions into dominant ones.

The tighter your control at the onset of a submission hold
the better you will be able to retain it against strong defensive countermeasures. If you have just enough mechanical tightness at

the onset to perform the lock, any defensive movement will take you below the threshold required for completion defensive movement always reduces the mechanical tightness of your submission hold. You need to over budget for the anticipated resistance. If you have twice the amount of mechanical tightness required to break the limb at the onset of the hold, and your opponent's defensive movements reduce this by a quarter, you will still be well above the threshold required for success. So right from the start, seek maximum mechanical tightness, so that the inevitable resistance will not be enough to stop you.

Looking forward to Texas!

This Saturday night in Austin Texas will be one of the biggest grappling events of the year - The Road To ADCC, a grappling super fight event using ADCC world championships rule set featuring the biggest names in the sport! Nicky Ryan will take on one of the toughest men on modern grappling - Dante Leon. Mr. Leon shocked the grappling world at the last world championships by defeating one of the greatest grapplers of the modern era - double ADCC silver medalist Lucas Lepri. Now he will face a Nicky Ryan in what is unquestionably the biggest test of the squad youngster so far! The show will use the special rules of ADCC finals matches - twenty minutes with any guard pulling subject to penalty - so there will be a lot of standing grappling alongside the ground work. Craig Jones was expected to headline with a match against ATOS superstar Lucas Barbosa but sadly he broke a bone in his hand during takedown practice and had to withdraw. The event is packed with great athletes. I can't wait to see main event - the great Kaynan Duarte, unquestionably one of the greatest grapplers on the planet, against Matheus Diniz, a master tactician who fears no one and who has the physicality required for such a huge match up! The brilliant technician Michael Musumeci will take on the mentally tough and athletically gifted Geo Martinez in a match up contrasting two polar opposite approaches to Jiu jitsu - this should be a tremendous match! There are other great matches as well! Gordon Ryan, myself and other squad members will teach a big seminar the night before on Friday and show the squad philosophy of Jiu jitsu - can't wait to see you all there and get back to Austin!! Keep your night open to see all these superstars in action!

Position and your mindset:
The ideal of Jiu jitsu is control leading to submission. The most well-known form of control is POSITIONAL CONTROL, where an athlete advances to the major scoring pins of Jiu jitsu which give him a greater ability to control and attack an opponent than the opponent has return fire. Your mindset when you achieve positional control tells you everything you need to know about yourself and your Jiu jitsu. When you get into a dominant pin, do you see that as AN END ITSELF? Or AS A MEANS TO AN END (submission)? If you celebrate the POSITION and see THAT as a victory, you will never express the ideal of Jiu jitsu. If you see the position merely as a step towards submission, then you have the mindset that produces the ideal of Jiu jitsu. Once you get to the position it's fine to take some time to establish control, tire an opponent, switch to another position etc. but inside your mind you must already be tirelessly searching how to go beyond the positional victory and on to the submission victory and thus to align yourself with the ideal of the sport.

When you first take a student into training, you try to make him see what you see, to think as you think, but ultimately the goal is to make him see more than you ever did and know more than you ever knew.

Glamor vs practicality: Everywhere is life we have to make a choice between an exciting, glamorous option vs a pragmatic, practical option. We have to choose between an exciting fast car versus a safe and reliable one, friends who can get you into fancy nightclubs and introduce you to excitement and fun versus a friend who always has your back no matter what. Jiu jitsu is the same. There are lots of exciting and fun elements that get our attention and there are some that are extremely important but don't get much attention. Probably the two least glamorous skill areas of Jiu jitsu are pin escapes and guard retention. Neither will result in highlight reels, yet your ability to perform all the more exciting aspects of Jiu jitsu is entirely dependent upon your ability to get out of bad pins and/or prevent them happening in the first place. You simply can't play an exciting game if you're being constantly held down and pinned. Make sure you devote a sufficient time in your training for the less glamorous but absolutely crucial aspects of the sport that may not be exciting in themselves, but which make the exciting aspects possible. Spend time getting out of pins and stopping opponents from passing - if you are starting out in Jiu jitsu I would prioritize these skills above all others.

Victory in Austin!!

Nicky Ryan had a great win at The Road to ADCC grappling super fight event tonight here in Austin, Texas! He took on one of the most talented 77kg grapplers in the world - Dante Leon - and won decisively with standing takedowns, scrimmaging up from guard position for wrestling reversals and some fine body lock guard passing. Unfortunately, midway through the match he badly hurt his knee entering another takedown - the same injury that prevented him from the Roberto Jimenez match earlier in the year. Well ahead on points, he decided to sit to guard and use his retention skills to hold Mr. Leon off until time ran out and took a decisive win. Obviously, we will have to get that knee checked out, but still, it was a fine win using his expanding skill set against a top ranked opponent. It was a great night of action hosted by Mo Jassim and Flo Grappling and great to see the athletes in the ADCC rule set again. Congratulations to Kaynan Duarte, Michael Musumeci and Roberto Jimenez who all took very victories tonight - the Jimenez/Ruotolo match was a like a highlight reel! Amazing work from all the athletes tonight. Thank you so much to the many people who came to the Gordon Ryan seminar last night! It was awesome teaching here in Austin and great to show our approach to Jiu jitsu in this great city! Hope you enjoyed the show!

Mats, memories and meetings:

I began teaching introduction classes under my sensei Renzo Gracie. As senior instructors left to create their own schools my teaching responsibilities grew. In 2001 MMA was a fringe sport trying to recover from a time when it was banned from television and decried as violent expression of "human cock fighting." Often, we would watch MMA from Japan where it was an accepted sport. One day in early 2001 was teaching private classes when a crew of Japanese athletes came in to train at Renzo's. They were doing grappling-based MMA training rather than Jiu jitsu. I recognized the main athlete as Caol Uno, a highly ranked athlete of that era who always fought with courage and skill and often survived terrible predicaments in his fights to come back to victory. Mr. Uno was in America for his bout with early MMA icon, Jens Pulver. He did a long and arduous workout and was suffering thirst. I went to front desk and got him some bottles of water and gave them to him. We didn't speak each other's language but his genuine sense of thanks was impressive. Almost twenty years later I was teaching a seminar with the squad in Singapore. After showing a technique I looked for my water bottle when Caol Uno came out of nowhere and offered me a bottle of water!! He was in the gym training for another fight in a few days - history repeating itself after two decades!! Once again lack of language didn't stop the feeling of heartfelt thanks - this time going in the opposite direction! This sport is amazing. Just a brief connection on the mats can form a bond that lasts far beyond what you'd expect! The best part was trying to explain to Nicky Ryan who Caol Uno was - Nicky was not even born at the time the first meeting happened!!

Start well end well:
When it comes to getting grip and/connection to an opponent - YOU MUST FACTOR IN EXPECTED RESISTANCE TO THAT

GRIP/CONNECTION. Every time you make a grip with your arms or legs you can expect resistance from a knowledgeable opponent. This resistance will loosen and weaken whatever grip or connection you've made. If you start with ADEQUATE grip/connection, that will resistance will immediately make it INADEQUATE - which will result in failure. If you start with PLENITUDINOUS grip/connection the expected resistance will lower to ADEQUATE level - which is enough to get the job done. Keep this in mind when fighting for grip and connection and success will come to you more often when coming to grips with tough opponents.

How far ahead do you think?
We always get told not to focus only on the move we are performing but always to look ahead to the next moves should the current one fail. So, if I'm attempting an arm bar from guard then I ought to be ready to switch to a triangle if it should fail, and then on to an omoplata should the triangle fail etc. it's natural to ask - how far out into the future should I be looking with my moves? Does it indicate that I am a better, more sophisticated Jiu jitsu player if I am thinking twelve moves ahead rather than only two or three moves ahead? I usually encourage students to think three or four moves ahead. Anything more than that becomes a little unrealistic as there are way too many variables that could lead to a totally new situation by the time that many moves have been completed in most cases in a competitive match against someone your own level. Plotting too many moves also has a negative effect. It tends to make us under value and under commit to the moves we are attempting here and now and over emphasize moves that haven't even occurred yet. This usually leads to unacceptably high failure rates with the submissions

we attempt. Limiting yourself to three or four move chains means you put a solid commitment to the move in front of you but have enough depth to continue attacks after initial failure for realistic periods of time. So, arrange your favorite moves in three shot combinations and you'll hit a sweet spot of realism and idealism - enough moves in a combination to break through strong defenses but not so many that you never commit strongly enough to finish any one of them.

Be quick to critique your own moves as you perform them.
Develop a clear sense of when they will work and when they will not. When you feel them begin to fail you will be able to read failure quickly and move to a second move more quickly than an opponent can follow with his defense and get a breakthrough. At the higher levels it's often not who moves first fastest that wins but rather who moves second fastest.

Scrimmaging up from bottom position:
So often when we practice Jiu jitsu we carry in our heads a strange "gentleman's agreement" that if you are the bottom player, you will remain in bottom position until you get a submission or a conventional Jiu jitsu sweep. This blinds us to myriad attacking opportunities that arise whenever space develops between you and the top player. This space can very often be used to come up off your back and into reversals based upon wrestling type movements normally associated with standing grappling. These score every bit

as effectively as the more conventional sweeps of Jiu jitsu and form an ideal complement to a traditional Jiu jitsu guard game, particularly when playing without a Gi. You don't have to be the best wrestler in the room to get them to work well for you. Often it is easier to get them to work because your opponent is distracted or caught out of stance due to the submission threat or an initial sweep attempt that breaks his balance. You will often surprise yourself by successfully using reversals from guard on opponents that you really struggle to take down in standing position. Look that sweep/submission/takedown interface in your guard game - the results may impress you!

End of an era:
It is with great sadness that I have to announce the breakup of the squad as a unified training and competition team. A combination of factors revolving around disagreements in physical location of a future school, personality conflicts, conflicting values and an inevitable tension between the team brand and the growing individual brands of members were the main factors. I am immensely proud of the tremendous effect the squad had upon the development and direction of our beloved sport over the years. I am extremely confident that all the various team members have risen in competitive ability, teaching skill and independent creativity that they will be highly successful wherever they choose to go - whatever happens their legacy is assured and their future very bright indeed. As for the future, it is still uncertain. Most of us still get along very well. I expect some will still train together and we will work together in future projects in accordance with our team philosophy, but no longer as a single unified room. I believe the split will have the

positive effect of creating a larger footprint for the team as they spread out and develop a wider influence. I always believed that the technical development of the team was best created by a tight, unified room, but at the end of the day human happiness outweighs medals and martial skill and it has become clear that some individual members would be happier in different locations. I would like to thank all the members of the squad for the tremendous effort and myriad sacrifices they made to build a team and legacy that will be remembered, in particular, Garry Tonon, Gordon Ryan, Craig Jones, Eddie Cummings, Nicky Ryan and Nick Rodriguez. I would also like to thank the many students who formed the room in which the squad developed and honed their skills; and thank you so much to all our faithful followers for your interest and support over the years - I hope and trust we can keep the project of refining our art going despite the changes - Thank you.

The impossible goal of seeking perfection

in Jiu jitsu performance is a fine metaphor for our lives in general. We all know we will stumble often and come up short at the end, but just as no matter how fast we ran as children, the rainbow always stayed well ahead of us, that didn't make it any less alluring or captivating; so, to on the mats. Whatever happened in your day, vexations, frustrations and disappointments, every training session is a chance to forget it all for a time and chase that impossible but fascinating goal. Keep yearning and keep learning, you'll never be perfect but you can perfectly imperfect.

In the gym you regret every minute of playing defense - it's uncomfortable, frustrating and unexciting. When the chips are down however, and you're in the battle of your life against a very dangerous opponent, you will relish the memory of every minute you spent working defense and wish only that you'd spent even more time in those uncomfortable, frustrating and unexciting positions. Don't skimp on defense - you only learn its value when you really need - and by then it's too late. Know its value early on and you will have a real advantage over your peers.

Why is guard position the most emphasized position in Jiu Jitsu?
When you look at all the various grappling arts you will see that the most distinctive facet of Jiu Jitsu is its heavy emphasis upon guard position. Many grappling arts such as wrestling do not have it all. Others such as Judo and Sambo have it but it is not heavily emphasized or seen as desirable. So why does Jiu jitsu make it the centerpiece of its game? There are several good answers you could offer. You might argue along the longs of tactical or historical considerations and certainly there are some very interesting possibilities there. I have always favored a more physical argument. Jiu jitsu has an ideal - the ability to control greater size and strength with lesser size and strength. Other grappling styles have the same ideal, but a different way of realizing it. Judo has this ideal and due to it being a predominantly standing art using balance breaking as its primary means of overcoming greater size and strength. Jiu jitsu does it primarily by MATCHING THE STRENGTH OF THE LOWER BODY AGAINST AN OPPONENT'S UPPER BODY WHERE EVER POSSIBLE. An opponent may be considerably

larger than you, but his arms will not be stronger than your legs. Guard position allows you to match your leg and hip strength against an opponent's arms and shoulders - a battle that a smaller, weaker person with skills can realistically win against a bigger stronger person. Among us human beings the difference between the strength and endurance of our lower body compared with our upper body is considerable - match your legs against a bigger opponent's arms and you're matching your stronger half against his weaker half - that's how smaller people can beat bigger people on the floor - and that's why I have faith in guard position as the basis of the bottom game.

Started from the bottom, now we're here:
Too often Jiu Jitsu players work with an odd "gentlemen's agreement" that one will be the top player passing and the other will be the bottom player working for conventional Jiu jitsu sweeps and submissions. This means that they miss out on myriad opportunities to come up from bottom positions into takedowns based on common wrestling movements and which are extremely effective in no Gi grappling. Interestingly, because the entire set up process is very different from standing wrestling you can sometimes even takedown/sweep opponents coming up from bottom that you ordinarily cannot take down in neutral standing position. It requires a sense of distance and a mindset that just because you STARTED in bottom position, you don't have to STAY in bottom position - that if the opportunity is there, you can change from conventional SEATED or SUPINE positions into KNEELING positions that allow quick shots into the opponent's legs. This is a relatively easy mindset and skill to adopt and can get great results in a short time.

Control first or submission threat first?

When attacking the back, we are normally always taught to establish position first, strangle second. There is a lot of wisdom to this approach. For most people, most of the time, it is the best option. Why? First, because position scores, and you being ahead on points means the opponent must now take greater risks to escape and get his own scores. Those risks will make him more vulnerable to subsequent attacks. Second, position allows you to make repeated attacks over time. So, if you experience initial failure you get to make second, third or fourth attempts at will until you achieve the breakthrough. Third, punishing positions like rear mount can fatigue an opponent over time and make later strangles easier. For these and other reasons it's usually a good idea to focus on securing the position first and worry about strangles later. However, one problem with this approach that often appears at championship level is that opponents are mentally and physically tough (won't fatigue or quit over time), tactically smart (often will prevent a score by denying a hook) and skilled at hand fighting defenses (can hold off many attacks over long stretches of time). In these cases, it is often better to attack the strangle in those vital half seconds BEFORE you establish the position as your opponent is primarily concerned with defending the position and will often leave the neck momentarily open. Interestingly, his panicked reaction to a strong initial strangle threat will often make the subsequent battle for position easier. Flicking your wrist under his chin very early on in the attack can be a good alternative strategy to employ in these situations.

Remember always that as a student of Jiu Jitsu
you are first and foremost a student of the human body. The deeper your knowledge of its strengths and weaknesses, the deeper will be your expression of Jiu Jitsu.

Two phase sweeps/reversals from open guard:
When we begin the study of Jiu jitsu we are taught a classical paradigm of guard sweeps that utilizes the great power of Gi grips along with a curriculum of traditional sweeps that take us directly from bottom to top position. In competitive no Gi matches however, we often have to make use of a messy, scrappy paradigm of guard sweeps that has two distinct phases in the transition from top to bottom. The first is a classic Jiu jitsu sweep that knocks an opponent down to his hands and/or hip. The inherently weaker grips of no Gi grappling however, make it very difficult to control a strongly resisting opponent during and after his fall. As the opponent tries to recover from the off balancing, we go into phase two - we tackle the opponent around the legs/hips/waist to secure a much more robust no Gi grip and scrimmage up into a takedown reversal. While it is not pretty to look at, this two-phase approach is very realistic and effective in competitive situations where your classic sweeps just aren't getting you the scores you need. Next time you're sweeping without the Gi - don't complacently relax as the opponent falls - be ready to scrimmage up from bottom and finish what you started!!

Know the strong points of each positional variation:

Jiu jitsu gives you a LOT of choice. Any given position has many variations within it - each of those variations has it good points and bad points. Each presents element's that suit your body type in some ways and frustrates it in others. Take guard position for example. There are dozens of different types of guard. Each different configuration offers different connection to an opponent and hence different possibilities for attack. It is important you understand that connection and its ramifications for your attack choice. Take closed guard for example. Its most important feature is that locks your hips on top of your opponent's hips so that even though your body as a whole is underneath your opponent's body, the most important part of your body, your hips, are on top of the most important part of your opponent's body - his hips. This has important ramifications. It means that any sweep or reversal that maintains that hip connection will result in a sweep directly to mounted position rather than merely a sweep to top position as is the case with most guard sweeps - after all, closed guard is essentially just an upside-down mount position as far as body connection goes. This insight tells you that almost any form of submission you can employ from mount will be applicable from guard - the set ups will be different given the change from top to bottom - but technique selection will be the same. It means that any form of go behind that gets you around and behind your opponent's arms will lead directly to rear mount. Knowing the most important feature of each given position in Jiu jitsu will give you the insights you need to direct your attacks better. Don't just associate a position with a list of attacks - look for its deeper mechanical basis and you will see further than your opponents.

One day far out in the future you will have to face the biggest Jiu jitsu challenge of your life.
You don't know who it will be and you don't know when it will be - but one thing you DO know is that your best chance at victory will always be to start here and now with the best PREPARATION you can. In a world of uncertainty that's something you can be sure of.

Legends:
One of my favorite aspects of Jiu jitsu is meeting legends of the sport. When I first began Jiu jitsu I was always impressed by the work of the Machado brothers. They all lived in California but were cousins of my sensei, Renzo Gracie, so we always thought of them as distant relatives. They exhibited Jiu jitsu of the very highest quality and were an inspiration to the Jiu jitsu world. Jean Jacques Machado was among the most brilliant ADCC champions of all time and Rigan Machado was widely considered as one of the very best athletes of his era and arguably the best. Certainly, as a beginner in the sport I learned a lot by observing their movement and match pacing which was very advanced. In fact, a move that is often associated with my students today - where from seated guard we trap both our opponents' feet from behind and sweep them backwards with a push from open guard position - I learned from Jean Jacques (people always ask me if I learned it from Marcelo Garcia, but no, it was Jean Jacques who I learned it from). Many years later at EBI ADCC and UFC events and where they were coaching or spectators, I would see Rigan, Jean Jacques or Carlos Machado from time to time (there were other brothers but I never met them). They were always the coolest guys and we'd talk about Jiu jitsu and crazy old matches they'd had back in the day! Thanks

to the brothers for their great role in the development and expansion of Jiu jitsu over the years - thank you for being legends in our sport.

Sometimes when you look at Jiu jitsu,
it just seems like a hopeless and disorganized tangle of thrashing limbs - but always remember that under that apparent chaos there are TWO THINGS that give Jiu jitsu direction - POSITIONAL DOMINANCE and SUBMISSION. Understand that no matter confusing or complicated it may seem there are only five dominant positions and around fifteen high percentage submissions in the game - as long as you're constantly searching and working towards those two end points you will be going forward. Keep your mind on the endgame and your Jiu jitsu will always have direction minute by minute however disorganized and disoriented it might appear second by second.

Grips - Imposing and denying:
Everything starts with grip in Jiu jitsu. Most of the gripping initiates with the hands, but given that the feet are an essential part of gripping when playing guard, they can sometimes initiate gripping as well. You can't do much in grappling until some form of grip is established. How that grip is established will usually determine all the next steps of the battle. Both athletes will try to impose their own grips while denying an opponent grip. This initial grip fight is one of the factors most responsible for determining the outcome of

the match as a whole - yet is largely ignored as a skill by most students since it is not visually interesting. I can tell within seconds of initiating contact with an athlete what his overall skill level is and what is his tactical plan just based on his gripping and grip sequences. Make sure your gripping game is consistent with your overall game. Make sure also that there is some subtlety in your gripping game. Your grip reveals a LOT about your intentions - so throw some fakery and deceit into your grips as well to make yourself less transparent. This game ends with submission - but it starts with grip.

When every round is tough –
keep going - there is a deeper skill to learn: The best time to learn nuanced skill is when your mind and body are fresh. Nonetheless there is a skill that you must learn that you will NEVER learn when you're fresh and rested. This is THE SKILL OF GRAPPLING WHILE YOU'RE EXHAUSTED. This is a truly important skill. Anyone can fight well when they're fresh - but it takes a special discipline to maintain your composure and decorum when you are close to collapse. You can only learn this through experience. There are subtleties to this aspect of the game. You must learn to pace yourself within whatever reserves you have left - to manage your dwindling resources and still get to your goals - to change your goals to stay within your endurance. All these are learned by putting yourself in duress. So next time your mind is screaming at you to sit out the next round - go back in. You will learn more about yourself in the next few minutes than you did in the previous decades before you learned to grapple. Those lessons will be vital for your development both on and off the mats.

A lesson from a young blue belt:

I think it's fair to see we all enter this sport with a lot of self-doubt. Your first few years is just a long story of getting your ass kicked every day at the dojo. As a result, it's natural to wonder if you'll ever be any good, if you'll ever be able to match the people currently crushing you, whether as a blue belt you'll ever be able to take on the upper belts. This weekend talented young Daniel Manasoiu, a nineteen-year-old blue belt went to The European Open, where Europe's best gets together to battle it out no Gi under ADCC rules. Most of the athletes are very experienced brown and black belts. Big Dan won double gold, both his weight division and absolute with his devastating submissions game - specializing of course in leg locks. I have always been impressed by the incredible sporting heritage and success of the Eastern European nations. I believe one day they will be a powerful force in the world of grappling. Big Dan is American but first-generation Romanian so he was very proud to go back to his roots and take double gold. It is a great lesson for all of us. That if you train hard, you can overcome higher belts and more experienced opponents who have been in the sport much longer. The only thing that counts on the mat is your skills, and if you work hard and intelligently, you can grow those faster than many people believe, so that your current doubts can be replaced by future triumphs. Well done Dan!

Make sure you're immune to your own poison:
An odd thing about combat sports is that quite often (not always) athletes who excel at a given move are themselves surprisingly vulnerable to that same move. This might be because everyone they train with us so fearful of that move that the athlete in question never gets to practice defending it himself. So, for example, when Garry Tonon fought Rousimar Palhares, a man greatly feared for his leg locks, I encouraged him to immediately attack Mr. Palhares's legs. If you have favorite moves - make sure you know both sides of them - attack AND defense. Only when you know both aspects can you rightly be described as a master of the position.

Tunnel vision:
One of the most natural and destructive human tendencies we have in the mat is tunnel vision. When we have an objective in our mind there is a powerful tendency to shut our eyes to other possibilities which may well be more promising. One of my tasks as a coach is to call out those other possibilities as they arise. The choice is still in the hands of the athlete - but at least he or she now works with a CHOICE of options rather than only one - and in a world where selection is done in seconds and can impact the outcome - that's an important thing. When you train there is always a voice there to open your peripheral vision - so train yourself to always have at least two options for every second-by-second moment of attack - you will immediately double your rate of success.

Intensity:
The sport of Jiu jitsu is ideally a mix of mostly relaxed efficiency mixed with spurts of ultra-high intensity at the moments where either a big score or a submission is being attempted. Learning to guard when to be relaxed and when to go hard is a huge part of your development. Remember always to put a cap on your intensity - both in terms of HOW OFTEN you go into maximum intensity level and HOW LONG you stay there. Mistakes with either will quickly get you exhausted and unable to go into overdrive when you really need it. The first skill you learn is to monitor your OPPONENT, but as you go further will find that it is just as important to monitor YOURSELF so that you do not get exhausted before you attain victory.

Sometimes skills carry over directly -
sometimes they carry over indirectly: Sometimes you learn a skill that you can see the moment it is taught to you that it will be immediately applicable to your game. So, for example, if you specialize in heel hooking and you learn a new and effective way of exposing a heel, you know that you'll probably be able to apply it very soon and it will fit in very well with what you already do. Other times the skills are applicable, but in a much less direct way. Even more extreme are the many law enforcement and military personal I teach. Sport Jiu jitsu is very removed from the world in which they operate where there are no mats, weapons are normal, they are dressed in body armor with a full kit that greatly restricts movement. Still, the skills are useful - it just requires more thought about modification and appropriate application, if understanding what needs to be changed for the different environment, rule set (or

total lack of rules) etc. There is a lot of useful knowledge out there that can benefit your game - just because it's not immediately and directly applicable to your game doesn't mean it can't be beneficial in some less obvious way - keep an open mind and you may well find that an insight you gained can be applied to your situation in ways that increase your performance.

Even the best move
applied at the best time can fail due to just a single mistake if the opponent is strong on defense. Aim for perfection in every aspect of execution - you can't close every door - but the more you do - the more success you will have. Don't be satisfied with good, aim for great in your areas of specialty in the game!

Developing a favorite move:
Jiu jitsu is not just a science of levers and fulcrums and centers of gravity; it is a deeply personal art of self-expression. In a world of millions of competing choices, you get to choose which moves will become yours and express yourself through them. It is crucial that you learn Jiu jitsu this way. The Japanese in their wisdom recognize the importance of this and term favorite moves "TOKUI-WAZA." You must develop YOUR tokui-waza. From these favorite moves will come most of your successes. Whenever you're in trouble they will be your shield. Whenever you struggle to get the breakthrough, they will be your hammer. As opponents learn that you have a favorite move, they will learn to counter it - forcing you to evolve

and improve your knowledge and performance of the move and to learn new, complimentary moves to supplement it - and thus your overall skill level increases like branches growing from the central trunk of a tree. This is one of the best ways to grow quickly in Jiu jitsu - and it all starts with developing some favorites - what will be yours?

Make it a battle of your legs
against your opponent's upper body and you will prevail even against bigger opponents and make it look effortless against smaller or same size opponents. An opponent might be considerably bigger and stronger than you overall, but his arms are not bigger and stronger than your legs. Learn to fight his arms with your legs and you will put yourself on a winning track. You can't always do it, but when you can it is a truly fine representation of the ideals of Jiu jitsu.

Fighting until the last:
In Jiu Jitsu it's natural to get a sense that a battle has been lost and stop fighting. Sometimes it's tactically smart to think this way - for example, you can recognize that one battle has been lost so stop fighting that battle so that you can reserve your forces for the next one. Other times however, you'll want to fight to the end and concede nothing. This is often the case with guard retention. Understand that until your opponent has completely cleared your legs and pinned your head and one shoulder down for three seconds - he has not passed your guard. That gives you a LOT of leeway for

last minute, last second scramble defense that can prevent a score and keep you in the game. This is the kind of spirit you usually want to exhibit in guard retention battles!

Vertebrates:

The most fundamental feature of our human bodies is our vertebrate nature - our bodies are completely dominated by our most basic structure - a spine connected to our skull. Everything is connected to this. Because the head is at the end of the spine and the spine functions as a lever - HE WHO CONTROLS THE END OF THE LEVER - THE HEAD - CONTROLS THE WHOLE BODY. There are many ways as to HOW you can control the head from standing and ground, top or bottom. There are even more variables as to WHEN you can control the head based on your position relative to your opponent. Never lose track of the fact that the best overall way to control a human is through their head. Look for it whenever possible and learn when it's available and when it's not. You can do it more easily when an opponent is wearing a Gi jacket since it functions like a rope around the neck, but there are plenty of great ways to do without a Gi also - either way - make it one of the primary goals of your grappling style.

Your first priority –

defensive soundness: I am sure on many occasions you have seen two completely untrained people fight each other. The first thing you notice is that neither is concerned with defense but instead they are totally preoccupied with their offense. As a result, the fight looks like it will be decided on a coin toss - whoever lands first will win. The first sign of expertise in combat sports is constant defensive awareness. GOOD FIGHTERS AND GRAPPLERS ALWAYS WORK ON THE ASSUMPTION THAT EVERY TIME THEY ATTACK THERE WILL BE IMMEDIATE COUNTER ATTACKS. As such they never enter into offense with an escape route and positioning that will either deny counter attacks or make them difficult. MAKE A HABIT OF DEFENSIVELY SOUND POSITIONING and you will remove the randomness of outcome that is the hallmark of untrained fighters and replace it with outcomes that heavily favor you. Enter, apply and finish every attack with defensively sound positioning and the outcome will be something you can count on rather than wish for.

Resistance:

We never really know for sure what moves our opponent will do in a match - but one thing we DO know for sure is that he will resist every one of OUR moves. Learning to OVERCOME and MOVE AROUND resistance is a lifelong study in Jiu jitsu. No one cares how beautiful your moves look with a cooperative training partner during drills - what really counts is how successful you are at applying them in a competitive setting on a skilled opponent who doesn't want to lose. This will require skills in SET UP. If you can disguise the entry to your moves in some way, then execution will be easier. It will require skill in COMBINING MOVES, if you can follow a failed move with a second or third follow up, your opponent will often fail to follow the change in direction in time and be caught. Learning to disguise your intent and work in combinations are the two best ways to counter resistance in all combat sports - Jiu jitsu is no exception. Be sure to imbed your power moves in creative set ups and combinations and the principle problem of sparring - overcoming resistance - will be much easier.

Hands:
Whenever you are working for the major upper body submissions - be aware that in the majority of cases, YOUR OPPONENTS FIRST DEFENSIVE MOVE WILL BE WITH HIS HANDS/ARMS. As such, IT IS PRUDENT TO BEGIN MOST UPPER BODY SUBMISSION ATTACKS WITH A DELIBERATE ATTEMPT TO TAKE OUT YOUR OPPONENTS ABILITY TO USE HIS HANDS DEFENSIVELY PRIOR TO COMPLETING THE SUBMISSION. It's a simple but important concept - DOMINATE THE HANDS AND YOU WILL USUALLY DOMINATE THE SUBMISSION OVERALL. Don't get tunnel vision on the submission. Remember that a skilled opponent will resist your attempt as soon as he identifies the danger. Take out the first defensive apparatus he can use and you will be a step ahead as you battle for completion.

Your mind is your greatest weapon –
but your legs are a close second: We've all had the disconcerting experience of grappling against someone far stronger than ourselves. It's a bad feeling when your opponent's hands easily peel off your best grips and pull out of your best holds. Whenever you feel outgunned in strength - it's time to use your basic knowledge of

the human body in your favor. No matter how much stronger your opponent's hands and arms may be than your hands and arms - his hands and arms are not stronger than your legs. Make it a fight of your legs against his arms and you can realistically beat stronger people. The best place for you start this study is submission holds that directly match your legs against an opponent's head and arm - and the triangle is king of this. Make it central to your training - and more importantly - central to your JIU JITSU MINDSET. THINK in these terms and you will begin to ACT in these terms, and then you may start to surprise yourself when grappling bigger and stronger opponents.

Learning to fly –
and fall: Even if you are a grappler who generally avoids standing position in favor of ground work, at some point you are going to get picked up and thrown hard into the mat - there is no getting around this. Learning to take the impact of a hard throw and get back into grappling with minimum fuss and interruption is very important. Failure to absorb the impact well will at best leave you discombobulated and easy to attack in the immediate aftermath of the throw and; at worst, get you some time in hospital. Beginners are usually taught some simple solo drills that do a good job of showing how to distribute the impact on to a big surface area of the body and direct that impact onto parts of the body well suited for hard impact - that is what will protect you from harm. At some point however, you have to go beyond the solo drills and actually get thrown if you are to be able to apply your knowledge under the pressure and stress of hard competitive sparring. I know many people who look great doling their solo break fall drills but who fall

badly in actual match conditions. The best way for beginners to bridge the gap between the basic solo drills and real-world hard throws is to start with one or both knees on the floor and have a standing partner throw you repeatedly so that you get the feel of being thrown fairly hard by real throws but fall only half the distance of a real throw and thus take less than half the impact (because you never fully leave the ground). This is a good way for beginner athletes to get to the next level of confidence in taking standing throws that can help people who started the game later in life and simply aren't used to getting thrown in a competitive match. Once this becomes easy for you it will be a lot easier to move on to being thrown from full standing position and your overall safety in hard training will be improved.

Why Gordon Ryan is the best no Gi mount player I ever saw:

Jiu jitsu is a game of position above all. At the top of the heap of the various positions are the mounts - front and rear. They both score the maximum points and you can argue as to which is the better of the two (in grappling I generally prefer rear mount over mount) but one thing is sure - they are both damn good. Of all the myriad athletes I have seen over the years the two best practitioners of the mounted position by a landslide were Gordon Ryan (no Gi) and Roger Gracie (Gi). It is worth asking - what makes Gordon Ryan's no Gi mount game so much better? The position seems pretty simple on the face of it. There aren't that many moves from there and most athletes know those moves by the time they're blue or purple belts. Lots of people get to the position, so what makes Mr. Ryan different? Well, I could list quite a few features, but I want to focus on the most important feature - the use of the LEGS as the primary connection and control mechanism of the position. When most people get mounted, they immediately focus their attention on the upper body. They fixate on chest-to-chest contact and connection through a crossface. This is fine, certainly these things can be very important, but never as important as what's going on downstairs at the legs. The primary connection is through your legs. You have many choices as to how that connection is held. Each choice will make in you strong in some ways, weak in others. Each choice will have important ramifications for how an opponent can escape and how you can shut down those escapes. Each choice will facilitate certain types of submission attacks and rule out others. Never lose track of the fact that the mount is just a guard position upside down and guard is just an inverted mount. Just as your LEGS are the basis of connection and control from guard - so must they be from mount. Just as you play with many alternative foot positions from guard, so must you do from mount. Just as you must get angle and head control with your legs from guard, so must you do from mount. This lower body focus must be your goal from mount.

Phases:

an odd thing about my career in Jiu jitsu is that it went through three very distinct phases. When I began I was a bouncer working in night clubs and only interested in Jiu jitsu as a self-defense skill. In time I became an instructor at my sensei Renzo Gracie's academy and taught Jiu jitsu to all, but was most known for my work on MMA grappling through my student Georges St Pierre. Mr. St Pierre was a super star and attracted many other great MMA athletes and grapplers. The emphasis accordingly was on no Gi grappling appropriate to MMA competition with a heavy emphasis on takedowns, top control and escapes. After that came a third phase when submission grappling became very popular and the squad rose to prominence. Interestingly, each phase was around a decade in duration. Here is a classic photo of an afternoon class at Renzo's probably around 2008. You can see Georges St Pierre, Roger Gracie, Romulo Barral, David Branch, my great unknown student Brian Glick, off camera is a very young Garry Tonon (he used to come in for MMA grappling with Tom DeBlass), Frankie Edgar, Rory MacDonald and Shawn Williams. It always brings a smile to my face when I think of those days - so many amazing people in one room battling towards their goals and helping others battle to theirs. I've seen so many changes over the years in the people and places around me and I am eternally thankful for the changes and evolution they have all created within me.

What's your next move?

When we begin Jiu jitsu our question is always "what move do I have to do to get out of this predicament?" As we grow in skill the new question becomes, "what move should I do to attack?" As you go further still the question you must constantly ask yourself is "what move comes next if this one should fail." The reality of beginner Jiu jitsu is that is most about escaping bad situations. Intermediate Jiu jitsu is most about learning skills to with which to attack. Advanced Jiu jitsu is mostly about the exchange of attack and counter against a highly skilled opponent who knows all the same moves you do and also how to defend them. As such, the great skill you need is not attack per se, but combinations and chains of attack working on the assumption that the first ones will usually fail and it will be the second, third or fourth that gets the breakthrough. Even when everything is locked in and the end seems assured - your mind should STILL be asking - WHAT'S NEXT IF THIS FAILS? Remember always that as a general rule in Jiu jitsu defense is easier than offense, so your offense must carry a greater degree of precision and persistence than a potential opponent counts on.

Angle: Mount and closed guard
are essentially inversions of each other (as far as positioning goes). As such, they have something important in common - they require a pivot of ninety degrees if you want to attack your opponent with arm bars. This perpendicular shift is the key to strong arm bar attacks from mount and closed guard. The main obstacle to this perpendicular shift is almost always your opponent's ELBOWS. It interesting how when we set a goal in Jiu jitsu, say an arm bar from guard, it turns out the most important precursor has nothing or little to do with the goal - but if that innocuous precursor isn't satisfied - the goal will never be reached. The only way to turn ninety degrees against a resisting opponent is get the elbow of the arm you wish to attack inside your hip. You have many favorite moves I am sure - be sure to clearly identify exactly what the essential precursors to all those moves are, so that you have a clear sense of what you have to accomplish before your favorite moves can work. This step-by-step approach is vital to your success and progress.

Vary your intensity:
Your first day sparring in Jiu jitsu was probably pretty similar to mine and everyone else reading this post - you locked up with your opponent and gave everything you had at maximum power until you quickly exhausted yourself and got finished. The path towards expertise is largely bound up with PACE and INTENSITY. It doesn't matter how well conditioned you are - if you go at maximum intensity for a length of time, you will get exhausted. The key is to understand that high intensity is only required for brief periods in Jiu jitsu, usually when either attacking or defending a potential score or submission. This is only a tiny fraction of the total time of any given match. The rest of the time you should be a state of relatively relaxed, but alert, calm. Learning to cycle between long stretches of calm and short bursts of high intensity effort is a huge part of your development and is the true key to endurance on the mat. The better you get at this skill, the longer you can train and the fewer injuries you will suffer. In addition, your sparring will become a lot more enjoyable as a side benefit. If you have a hard time playing calm, make a note to stop in certain positions where you feel you can recharge and compose yourself, then as you improve, stretch those positions out more and employ more positions. Make it your goal to spend 70-80% of a match in a fairly calm state so you can save yourself for the 5-10% where the match is won and lost.

The magic of angle:
Understand this - any time you are engaged with an opponent, any defensive stance he takes is predicated on the current angle between him and you (usually you are directly in front of each other at the onset of engagement) - ANY CHANGE OF ANGLE ON YOUR

PART RENDERS THE OPPONENTS DEFENSIVE STANCE NULL AND VOID. In short, CHANGE OF ANGLE CHANGES EVERYTHING. If you can move to a new angle - DOORS THAT WERE PREVIOUSLY SHUT ARE SUDDENLY OPENED TO YOU - NOW is the time to attack!

You don't have to rush:

There are some times in Jiu jitsu where both you and your opponent know what you want to do. Attack will be more difficult know since your opponent will be putting himself in a strong defensive position. It's tempting to rush it - perhaps if you get the move into operation fast enough you'll get there before his position is set. Maybe, maybe not. Often a better way of doing things is stop and then let the opponent relax a little as he assumes you believe the move will no longer work against his defensive position - and then just as you feel him relax - go hard back into the move. This waiting game can be a great tactic in an apparent deadlock - make sure you learn to relax in sparring you can think and act in this tactical fashion rather than just as fast and hard as you can.

The relationship between POSITION and TIME:

From your first day in Jiu jitsu you were told that position is the most valuable commodity in Jiu jitsu. The usual reason given for this is that superior position allows you to attack without fear of an opponent being able to attack you. Certainly, this imbalance of attacking opportunity is a very important reason, but there is another. Position gives you the luxury of TIME. Once a dominant position has been attained, you can create pressure over time. You can attack and FAIL multiple times - IT DOESN'T MATTER. As long as the POSITION doesn't fail, it doesn't matter whether the first, second or third or fourth attempts at submission fail - just try again until you succeed - as with every failed attempt your opponent gets more tired, making the subsequent attempt more likely to break through. POSITION MAKES TIME A WEAPON, and of all the weapons at your disposal this often proves to be the dangerous of them all.

Alignment and misalignment:

The human body relies on good alignment to produce whatever strength it is capable of. When you watch champion Olympic weightlifters put up their mind-boggling lifts you can see the near perfect alignment of their bodies throughout the lift is what enables them to put up weights that would crush the rest of us. In Jiu jitsu too we need alignment when we want to be strong and efficient. Good posture makes the moves of Jiu jitsu easy. The flip side of this is that when we attack an opponent - THE ATTACK MUST ALWAYS BE AN ATTACK ON THE OPPONENTS POSTURE. If you can put your opponent into a forced, unnatural, contorted position, he will find it very difficult to defend himself. With the spine misaligned it's very difficult to even begin an effective defense, let alone complete it. Whenever possible look to take your opponent's body out of alignment to double the effectiveness of your attacks!

Pressure:
Pressure over time is the single greatest determinant of victory. It is rare to beat someone your own skill level quickly and easily - it can happen - but not often. Usually, it will be pressure over time that breaks an opponent to a point where they mentally accept defeat. Don't be upset when your moves fail - every attempt creates pressure that drains an opponent - each failure adds up over time and compounds upon the next until a breakthrough is reached and victory will be yours.

When you're close to a win you've got two options - speed or control: There are quite often situations in Jiu jitsu where you are close to total victory - say for example, when you are starting to apply a rear strangle, or when you have an opponent totally immobilized in a tight ashi garami with the heel exposed - or in this case with Georges St Pierre, a locked in arm bar. Your basic choice now is this - you can either rush to apply the finishing move and get it completed before the opponent can get himself defensively organized, or, you can take your time and control your opponent's movement so that you can make adjustments and even multiple finishing attempts over time to get the breakthrough. Both can work. As a general rule, however, I favor the control option. My reasoning is that speed options are almost always more likely to injure students in training and time lost in training makes victory in competition less likely. More importantly, speed creates momentum and looseness that can be used by a crafty opponent to aid an escape. Unfortunately, the speed options almost always prevent you from switching to the second or third attack option because everything is put into the quick application of the first attempt. Control methods allow multiple attempt and combination attacks that tend to do better at the higher levels. Speed attempts tend to work well up to a certain level or not work at all. You need to be able to apply both, as you may be attempting the move with very little time left on the clock or in a rule set that gives very limited time to attack (e.g. Judo), but if time is available, make sure you can work at controlled pace that enables you solve any puzzles the opponent presents to you, work through multiple attacks and variations before getting to the finish.

What are you known for on the mat?

In everyday life I am sure you are known by those around you to have a certain image of personality that is distinctively yours and which makes you recognizable to them. For example, you might be known as someone who likes fashion, or cars, or fishing or some activity or point of view that characterizes you. One of the most important elements in your development in Jiu jitsu is to develop your own Jiu jitsu image or personality that characterizes your Jiu jitsu game. Once you have this people will have certain expectations about you on the mat. YOU CAN EXPLOIT THESE EXPECTATIONS TO ADVANTAGE. If you are known as a dangerous back attack specialist, opponents will be very reticent about exposing their back to you. This will usually create defensive over reactions that you can use to win. If they focus on turning to face you to prevent back exposure, they will be easier to attack with guillotines, Darce and anaconda strangles. If they glue their back to the ground defensively, they will be very vulnerable to north/south strangles etc. Your image and reputation are important in this regard. It will influence how people behave around you, and their behavior will be predictable based on what you know about what they believe - and that is exploitable! So - what are you known for on the mat?

Everything important you ever do in Jiu jitsu will be done against strong resistance - be sure to factor this resistance into all your calculations BEFORE you make your move.

Start small, with a plan of how to take it all:
When you first come out to grapple with your opponent, the general pattern is to start with minor grips - usually starting at the hands or head. From there you work to increasing amounts of body contact and control. Because control is generally much easier on the ground than it is standing, the action typically transitions to the floor, where the idea is to get ever increasing amounts of body contact in ever increasing amounts of positional dominance. Make sure you realize this is a step-by-step process. Don't try to take too much too early. Start with the small actions of gripping hands and head and build from there. Trying to grab too much too early makes you easy to counter attack. Work progressively towards your goals and don't skip steps unless the opportunity is completely open (and even then, be aware it could be a trap). You will probably have to repeat this process many times over the course of a tough match - get used to it - it is the way of all Jiu jitsu.

Jiu jitsu is a series of exchanges
that begin with contact and end with separation - these are repeated over time until there is a result. This is important; it means that every time you re-engage, there is a chance for advantage if you engage on your terms. If you start most of the engagements on your terms, you will probably prevail over time. Every time you break contact and come back to re-engage, come back with a plan and act quickly on it as you approach. Don't just lazily step towards the opponent and complacently come to grips. Have a sense how you will gain advantage from the moment of contact every time and you will steadily wear down even the toughest opponents.

Open guard - so many possibilities –
don't restrict yourself: So many people start their open guard play with the idea that as the guard player, they have to stay on the back or buttocks until they get a sweep or submission. This is absolutely not the case. You will never maximize your potential in bottom position open guard until you get comfortable with the idea of getting up from your back or buttocks and coming up into reversals. This is even more so when training no Gi. In live sparring against someone your own size and skill level it is very difficult to sweep cleanly or submit decisively. Most attempts fail. It is crucial that you be able to follow a failed sweep or submission with a reversal where you scrimmage up from bottom and come to your knees and/or feet and finish by taking your opponent down and taking top position. The same is true in situations where you have an opponent who stays out of range of your primary guard attacks. You need to threaten coming up from bottom into takedowns to cover distance and force the pace from bottom position. In response your opponent will have to stuff the takedowns - this gives you the perfect opportunity to gain the connection you need for more conventional guard sweeps and submissions. In this way you can create a dynamic and attacking open guard game that can threaten opponents at every range and where you control engagement from bottom position. Remember, just because you START on you back or buttocks doesn't mean you have to STAY there. Play with a wider array of body postures and you'll be rewarded with a wider array of attacks across a wider array of scenarios.

Last mission in Puerto Rico:
I will be teaching a seminar in Puerto Rico on September 19. I am sad to be leaving the Island. Though there were obviously some sad elements to our time here, there were many more great ones. I will be eternally grateful to the many friends we made here and who generously gave time and resources to help us in our time in Puerto Rico. 100% of the money made in this seminar will go to gyms who let us train on their mats with no expectations of reward and to the Puerto Rico Jiu jitsu federation to help fund competitions for the many talented young athletes in the Island to show their skills in the future. We have greatly enjoyed showing our approach to the game in Puerto Rico over the last year and I look forward to a last chance to showcase it to a wider audience. ¡Deseandoles lo mejor! ¡Nos vemos ahi!!

The enemy advances, we retreat.
The enemy retreats, we pursue: In the ebb and flow of guard play, opponents will sometimes pressure forward and sometimes recede - it's is crucial you be able to follow that movement to advantage. So often when opponents move back, we stop moving and wait for them to come back to us. This is a missed opportunity. When they disengage it is the perfect time to surge forward and actively come up from bottom position and take your opponent down. Don't think that because you aren't a wrestling specialist that this kind of tactic won't work for you. It's generally much easier to perform many forms of takedown under these circumstances because your opponent's stance is usually compromised. Most Jiu jitsu players are very effective dealing with opponents driving forward into their

guard - make sure you are equally effective when they pull away in the opposite direction.

Always look to create a viable threat to your opponent whenever possible:

One of the biggest determinants of how your opponent will behave in a match overall, and at a critical juncture of a match in particular, is his THREAT ASSESSMENT of you. If he doesn't find you threatening at all, he will confidently attempt his moves. If on the other hand, he is strongly intimidated by you, he will be very reticent to attempt any but his absolute best moves and only when he feels it is safe to do so. Your opponent's willingness to move is a direct reflection of the level of threat he feels. Note how Georges St Pierre immediately threatens a strangle when he gets behind Gordon Ryan. Even if the threat isn't particularly strong, it will keep an opponent honest and force him to restrict his hands to a passive, defensive role. Most of those defensive roles are very predictable, which means you will have the tactical advantage in an ensuing hand fight. Always seek to create a level of threat that gets your opponent's attention - without it he will move much more freely and prove to be a more difficult adversary.

You're in a winning position –

now is not the time for excitement: It perfectly natural and understandable that you should get excited when you get to a winning position against a tough opponent. However, getting excited won't make it easier to finish. Now is the time for calculation and remembering the skills needed to finish the job. Stay cold and dispassionate and work methodically, the same way you would to solve a math problem - did getting excited or emotional ever help you solve a math problem? No - and it won't help you solve a Jiu jitsu problem either. Save your excitement for after the job is complete and you will experience excitement a lot more than if you let it creep in too early.

In a tough match you might only get one shot at victory...

better to be damn good at a few moves than average at many. Nobody remembers the moves that ALMOST worked - they only remember the moves that DID work. You want enough diversity of moves to cover the whole body, but not so many that you never really master any of them.

The basis of our open guard game –

the hook sweep (sumi gaeshi): The most versatile and effective sweep from open guard whenever an opponent is on their knees is, in my opinion, the hook sweep sumi gaeshi. It takes very little athletic ability, works both against and for all body types, and if the sweep should fail it leads directly into devastating leg locks since it is based on inside control. It can be done from almost any grip, it is easy to perform on both sides and you can switch rapidly from one side to another. There aren't many moves that I demand my students get good at - generally I try to encourage students to make their own choices - but sumi gaeshi is one of them. All of my senior students excel at it - you should too!

When you can get the upper body and the lower body facing in opposite directions,

you will generally dominate the top passing, pinning and pressure game. The two most powerful means of controlling the human body are the head and hips. If you can control both AND make them face in opposite directions, you truly put an opponent under pressure and he will find it very difficult indeed to stop you advancing to your next objective.

Getting ready for Austin Texas!

Gordon Ryan, Garry Tonon and I are getting ready for a big move to Austin Texas to begin teaching and training. I will teach a seminar here in Puerto Rico to raise money for local Jiu jitsu schools who supported us in our time here - it will be sad to leave the Island but I'm excited for the future. Going to Texas was always fun adventure for competitions - now it will be to make a home! Initially we will teach out if a small local school Renzo Gracie Austin, but we will start scouting for our own place as we become more familiar with the city. The fun part will be re-learning how to drive! I have not driven a car since 1991! I will have to get a driver's license like a teenager and learn to handle a modern car! I am pretty sure I will end up in some kind of vehicular disaster in the first week! Can't wait to get in the ground next week and start the journey to make Texas a Jiu jitsu powerhouse!

There are many measures of dominance in Jiu jitsu.
You have a dominant grip, balance domination, dominant angle, dominant position - but no single situation brings together so many aspects of dominance in grappling as getting behind an opponent. Seek it always. Hunt for it, fight for it - get it. Once you do, the game is so much easier for you and so much harder for your opponent.

Don't just attack the submission –
attack his base of support AND the submission and you'll double your chances of success: It hard enough to defend a well applied submission hold at the best of times - it's considerably more difficult when you've been knocked down to an awkward position from where you have no ability to apply strength or movement. Make use of this insight whenever you can. If you catch an opponent in a good lock - look immediately to go the extra distance and lock them out if their base of support so that they have TWO tasks - they have to defend the submission hold AND recover their base - the former is not possible until they perform the latter. This will give you a much greater chance of finishing them than just the hold itself.

Last day in Puerto Rico:
I had a great time today teaching a seminar here in Puerto Rico to benefit local Jiu jitsu schools and associations running competitions for local athletes. It's been an amazing experience watching some of the local Jiu jitsu athletes learn and improve this last year. Today we went over many ways to control and finish from back positions - a favorite theme in my teaching. Tomorrow morning, I will fly out to Austin Texas to start in a new locale and doubtless new adventures. Thank you to all the people who helped us train and prepare for competitions this last year in Puerto Rico!

First night in Austin Texas!
I flew into Austin this afternoon and went to teach at Renzo Gracie Austin tonight. It was fun going over back control techniques and tactics with an enthusiastic group of locals we will be teaching there while we get situated and organized and build our own place. I've always been impressed by the way change creates new outlooks and evolution in all of us - I'm sure the change will be a good thing and create a strong future. Tomorrow morning it's back to the mats for more!

The most fundamental forms of control over the human body will
always be control over the HIPS and the HEAD. Interestingly, in most cases you have to choose one or the other (there are some powerful exceptions). In most cases of top positional control, we

start with the hips and progress to the head, since the hips are typically closer. Make a deep study of hip control and head control and your game will improve greatly.

Positions for less athletic people:
A word that gets thrown around a lot in Jiu jitsu bus "athleticism." No one ever tries to define what they mean by this but generally it refers to an athlete's potential for movement - how fast they can move, what range of motion can they move through, how far they can move via running or jumping and for how long etc. In general, movement is aided by space that permits greater freedom of movement. Any kind of physical encumbrances that reduce movement potential is the enemy of athleticism. This provides an important general rule - THE MORE CONNECTION THERE IS BETWEEN YOUR BODY AND YOUR OPPONENTS, THE MORE YOU WILL REDUCE HIS ATHLETICISM. So, if you are older, slower, and just plain less athletic than your opponent - you want to maximize connection between your body and his to undermine his athletic advantage. So, the best positions for older, slower athletes to work successfully against younger, faster, more explosive, more flexible opponents are those that put the maximum area of your body in contact with his. Arguably the best example of this from bottom position is half guard. This creates very significant connection between the top and bottom player which has a great slowing and holding effect that can be used to undermine faster and more athletic opponents. Next time you feel physically outgunned underneath an opponent, try locking him up in half guard and see if you can take the pace down to a level that works in your favor instead of his.

Don't tolerate controlling/dangerous grips:

Oftentimes in Jiu jitsu you will feel an opponent get a good grip that feels like it controls you in some way that signals danger - a strong passing grip for example. Don't accept it - peel it off immediately to deny the advantage. You don't want to degenerate into a negative player who only focuses on grip denial at the expense of offense, but still, you have to take care of defensive concerns early before they become insurmountable problems, even if means backing off the offense for a short time.

Hands and feet:

when you use your arms to grab something you will usually use your hands as the connection to the object you are grabbing. So, if you want to pick up your briefcase - you will use your hand to grip the handle and your arms (in unison with other body parts) to do the lifting - the arms do the heavy work, the hands provide the connection. The legs and feet operate in a similar way from open guard position. In most cases, your legs do the heavy work, but the feet provide the connection to the opponent. Knowing this, when you are passing open guard, you must be mindful to control your opponent's feet as much as possible and seek to prevent them connecting effectively to your body (usually your legs). Foot control is essential to success. If the opponent's feet can connect securely to you, he will be able to use his legs very effectively to cause you many problems; but if the feet can't make effective connection, it will be more difficult for the legs to play an effective role. So, when passing

- MONITOR HIS FEET and try to prevent them connecting solidly to your legs. You'll have a much easier time imposing your passing game when you do so.

When grappling strong opponents sometimes it feels like their arms are like iron bars - but I promise you - if you can put an opponent's hand behind their back, even the strongest arm will feel weak. Exploit this physiological fact whenever you can!

Creating a threat:

How your opponent behaves towards you in a match is closely tied to whatever perceived threat level he believes about you. The higher his assessment of your threat level - the more conservative and reserved he will be in his actions around you - the less risks he will take as he engages with you. It is important therefore, that you take every opportunity to create attacking threats at all times during a match. Make sure that your defensive skills are closely followed by counterattack and that any indecision on his part is ruthlessly attacked by you. Positional threat is good, but submission threat usually creates a higher threat level, so make sure you have some favorite submission attacks for every scenario.

If you can trap an opponent's head and arm between your knees,

you will immediately be in position to attack the upper body with submissions. The ideal of Jiu jitsu is always to control greater strength and aggression with lesser strength and aggression. There are different ways to express this ideal - but one of the very best is to match the strength of your legs against an opponent's arms. This is a battle you can consistently win even against much stronger opponents. A simple and extremely effective way to do this is to clamp your opponent's head and one arm between your knees while taking an angle. This opens the door to arm bars, triangles, kimuras, omo plata - even leg locks if you know what you're doing. It immediately turns a passive or neutral bottom position into a highly advantageous one - look to get there as often as you can!

The stronger your initial attack –
the easier your follow up attacks: It's rather rare in top level Jiu jitsu to smash through your opponent's defenses on the first attempt and get the score. Usually it involves elaborate sets ups, fatiguing pressure over time or combination of moves to get a breakthrough. When it comes to combinations, a weak first attack is unlikely to evoke a sufficient reaction from a talented opponent to set up a good combination. Worse still, it may be strongly countered. You want a powerful first attack that throws your opponent into a totally defensive mindset and evokes predictable defensive reactions that you can capitalize upon. Don't hang back from the opening attack even though you know it's just a ruse to set up the subsequent attacks - go in hard to create the reactions you need to make the second, third or fourth attack score!

Speed:
Speed is a wonderful attribute in combat sports. In Jiu jitsu it is probably less important than it is in most other combat sports because most of the action is on the floor where speeds are always much slower than standing position. Nonetheless a very quick opponent definitely creates unique problems even in Jiu jitsu. However, what if you aren't particularly quick? What are you to do? Understand this - speed of body is great but speed of DECISION MAKING is better. Why? Because if you can make quick mental decisions, you can build ANTICIPATION into your game and anticipation will create an artificial speed advantage - not because it makes you faster but because it enables you to START THE RACE EARLIER. If you don't have the fast body - TRAIN YOURSELF TO HAVE THE FASTEST MIND THAT CAN IDENTIFY A

SITUATION AND MAKE A DECISION BEFORE YOUR OPPONENT HAS STARTED MOVING.

Weight vs weight distribution:
Don't let anyone fool you - weight is a big factor in combat sports and fighting. There is a reason why there are weight divisions. As a general rule between two athletes of roughly equal skill, the advantage will go to the bigger heavier athlete. Nonetheless there are some things you can do to make an opponent's weight work in your favor. Understand that if you can make an opponent carry his own weight - EVERY POUND THAT HE CARRIES IS A POUND THAT YOU DON'T HAVE TO CARRY - and that means a heavy man can be made to feel light, even if only briefly - that's enough to launch an attack! When underneath opponents in guard actively seek to off balance them to get their hands on the mat carrying weight. As their arms carry the weight of their upper body it will suddenly become much easier for you to move and manipulate their remaining body weight into submissions and sweeps. Remember - it's not just about how much your opponent weighs - but rather what percentage of his weight is actually on you - that determines your ability to engage him effectively.

Negate first –
attack second: Jiu jitsu can be a very scrappy game at times - especially when you and your opponent are launching attacks on each other at the same time. It's not wrong to do this; it can certainly

make for exciting and entertaining matches, but it's hard to develop the control and focus needed to score or finish on tough opponents when you are simultaneously attacking each other because you're worried about defense at the same time you're trying to conceive of offense. Often, it's a better approach to first shut down an opponent's ability to attack you with subtle positioning of your limbs and body before even thinking about your own offense. As your opponent's attacks falter, you will be able to slow things down and focus on what you want to do.

When your opponent's goes to initiate movement,
you've got two choices - either try to STOP the movement or GO WITH the movement. Both approaches are very effective - which one you choose in a given case will depend on the circumstances of that case - which one you choose in general will be determined by your body type and personality. One is not better than the other, but they do amount to very different expressions of Jiu jitsu. Garry Tonon was a master of FOLLOWING an opponent's movement - Gordon Ryan was a master of STOPPING an opponent's movement. Which do you generally prefer?

What was the first guard you learned?
Everyone agrees that guard position is one of the absolute foundations of Jiu jitsu. The heavy emphasis on guard play is probably the single most distinctive part of Jiu jitsu that separates it most from the other grappling arts. There are many types of guard

- which did you learn first? Most students begin with closed guard. There are good reasons for this. Closed guard represents one of the great ideals of Jiu jitsu - the ability to attack while not being oneself open to the opponent's attack - an opponent can't attack you with passes or submissions until he first opens your guard. However, many students struggle to actually apply the major moves from closed guard as the position overall often feels very unfamiliar and unnatural to a beginner. I often find that beginners do better as far as effectiveness from bottom position is concerned with half guard rather than closed guard. So, when it's time to teach bottom position to a raw beginner, try using closed guard to illustrate important concepts and half guard to make them effective in sparring in minimum time.

Memory:
The great challenge of Jiu jitsu learning is not how much you can learn - it is HOW MUCH YOU CAN RECALL UNDER STRESS. That is what matters. As such, memory and retention are among the most important factors in your progress. Everyone learns and remembers differently. Some learn and retain best with WRITING - that was always my favorite method; others never write a thing and have other methods, repetition, a seminal imprinting experience that burns the knowledge into their memory - whatever works for you. If you ARE the type that favors writing as a memory aid, you don't need to write everything you practiced down in excruciating detail every day. Just note the main ideas that were new in bullet point form. If it's a move that you learned, just write the two or three most important elements in order of importance. If it's a concept, describe its value and main applications that apply to you. Even if

you never read those notes again in your life, the mere act of focus and writing has a good clarifying effect on your thinking that will carry over into your grappling and overall thinking about the game. If you are ever injured and off the mats for a time, try writing as a temporary substitute for mat time and see how much you can recall and how clearly you can expound it. You might be surprised at how it helps you when you return.

Pinning:
The notion of pinning is central to almost all forms of grappling. In sports like wrestling and judo, pinning can end a match just as submissions do in Jiu jitsu. Jiu jitsu approaches pins from a very unique perspective - pins are understood to derive their value from their FIGHTING value. Only pins that prevent and opponent using their legs to defend themselves and enter into sweeps and submissions are acknowledged - so the first prerequisite is that you get completely past your opponent's legs. The other guiding idea is that you should be able to create an asymmetry in attacking potential - an ability to strike or submit an opponent far more readily than he can return fire. The more this asymmetry is exhibited, the better the pin. Learning to get to, maintain, move from one pin to another and attack from a pin is the centerpiece of the top game in our sport. Work first on MAINTAINING a pin against resistance - that's the first skill of pinning. Then work on moving smoothly from ONE PIN TO ANOTHER (and back if necessary) without being put back in guard - that's your second skill. Once you've gotten strong in these two skills, it's time to move to the third - attacking from pins with submissions. This can be frustrating at first because you usually have to relinquish the pin

itself to do so, but it represents the pinnacle of pinning so it's a hurdle you must jump!

The single biggest demand of Jiu jitsu -

use your legs as the centerpiece of your grappling game: The single most distinctive feature of Jiu jitsu as a grappling style is the degree to which it emphasizes the use of your legs as the main weapon to use against your opponent. The entire bottom game is based around guard position where you grapple your opponent's body with your legs. The top game is based around getting to three pins, mount, rear mount and knee on stomach where your legs connect you to an opponent's hips and torso. The upper body pins that don't involve legs - side and north south - don't even score. The most extreme example of legs as a weapon is the use of triangle strangle holds. The biggest obstacle every beginner in the sport faces is the fact that in everyday life we mostly use our legs for locomotion and not much else, so when we are suddenly asked to perform complex tasks with our legs we struggle. Developing strong suppleness and dexterity in your legs is thus of the utmost importance for every beginning student. Just practicing entering triangles with no hands is a wonderful way to start your journey into grappling first and foremost with your legs. However, you start that journey, how far you progress on it will determine how far and how fast you go.

What do the three most desired positions in Jiu jitsu have in common?

The two most dominant positions in Jiu jitsu are mount and rear mount. The best position when underneath an opponent is guard. What do all three have in common? YOU CONTROL AN OPPONENT'S HIPS AND TORSO BETWEEN YOUR KNEES. This allows an extraordinary amount of control and also the ever-present opportunity for the best submissions in the sport. Make it a habit to line up with an opponent and control him between your knees. This fulfills the Jiu jitsu ideal of grappling an opponent with your legs first and upper body second.

One move - many variations:

When we begin Jiu jitsu we talk about a given move in the singular - we talk about an "arm bar." As you develop you come to realize there are other variations of the arm bar - they are still arm bars insofar as they share the same basic mechanics - but the applications and positioning are quite different. All the major moves of Jiu jitsu have this feature and it is crucial for your development that you understand each of the variations and how they relate to each other. This is a BIG part of what expertise in the sport means. As the skill of your opponent's increases you will be required to show ever increasing knowledge of the nuances of variations and switching between them in order to defeat determined and skillful resistance. This kind of nuanced understanding of the variations is what you will require the further into the sport you go.

Pressure: when we think of winning in Jiu jitsu
we typically think in terms of MOVES. If a move is performed flawlessly, it wins a match. In reality however, we rarely perform moves flawlessly against the strong resistance of an opponent who has the similar knowledge, skill and size to ourselves. Typically, what determines winner and loser is PRESSURE OVER TIME. it is the ACCUMULATION of moves performed to a level that stresses an opponent that wears him down first physically and then mentally. As time passes his ability to counter your moves deteriorates faster than your ability to perform them. Learning to use pressure as a weapon is perhaps the single biggest factor in your effectiveness on the mat. You START Jiu jitsu learning MOVES, but you will FINISH it learning to impose and maintain PRESSURE.

Finishing grip first or control grip first?
There are some submission holds that involve a certain grip associated with the submission, for example a rear naked strangle involves a strangle hand around the neck, a heel hooks a wrist under the heel. Without that grip the submission would never occur. In addition, they require a control grip. In the case of a rear strangle it's usually the rear mount itself with your legs as hooks locking you in place, in the case of the heel hook it's whatever ashi garami variation you've chosen. The question is - which comes first? In the majority of cases the control grip ought to come first. It will slow an opponent down and give you the ability to focus on getting your finishing grip in place. In this photo you can see Garry Tonon has established ashi garami control first to lock on to an opponent's hips and now he can fight to get his wrist to the heel. At the higher levels however, there are good reasons to sometimes switch the order - usually because

opponents have highly developed defensive skills. Sometimes slipping the strangle hand in first and then beginning a strangle to distract an opponent will allow you to then slide into rear mount uncontested. Similarly, with a heel hook. Exposing the heel and getting your wrist to the heel first and then sliding into your favorite ashi garami will sometimes allow you to bypass the whole hand fighting phase of leg locking and grant you faster, cleaner finishes. Understand that usually the conventional method of control first, submission second is the way to go, but let that blind you to other possibilities when circumstances change.

Hands:

Almost everything we do in grappling begins with the hands. Our hands are weak compared with the rest of the body, but they are dexterous and fast moving. In truth they don't have to be that strong since their real function in grappling is as CONNECTORS. Our hands connect us to an opponent and the big muscles of the legs, hips and back do the heavy work. Nonetheless, without that connection through hand grip we wouldn't be able to apply force into an opponent with the rest of our body. As such, when it's time to shut down a dangerous opponent's ability to attack us in grappling - HAND CONTROL is among the best methods. If you can strip away an opponent's grip, trap his hands in place and/or frustrate his attempts to reestablish a lost grip, you can render his grappling skills null and void. Learn to distinguish when a hand grip is liable to cause you problems and if it is, take the time to nullify or remove it, then you can set your own positive grips and focus on your offense.

One of the biggest inhibitors of progress in Jiu jitsu
is a disproportionate preference for either top or bottom position at the expense of the other. Only when you see them as complimentary parts of a whole will your game have the uninterrupted flow required for great Jiu jitsu performance.

Got a good position?
Get a better one! Don't be satisfied with good when great is readily available. There are lots of good positions out there, but only a few great ones. Very often the transition from good to great is quite easy. Nothings beats getting behind an opponent. Next time you're doing well, ask yourself if you could be doing still better - usually the answer the yes. Don't hesitate - take that next step and turn good into great.

The other fellow:
Many years ago, I was in a UFC warm up room getting an athlete ready for competition. As the athletes get ready with exercises and drills, they get their hands wrapped by the professionals. It's fascinating watching a good hand wrapper go to work. They wrap with a precision that makes your hands feel like two steel encased weapons of war. As the wraps were being applied a young athlete was noisily expressing his approval and delight as his hands were

encased in gauze and cotton. "Man! My hands feel like two bricks! Anything I hit I will go right through!" He stood up upon completion and smashed one hand into his other and growled as he felt the heavy power the wraps gave him. "I could punch a hole in the wall now! If I hit him with these - he's sleeping!! I feel like a damn super hero!" The hand wrapper looked at him and quietly said, "very good - just remember that right now in another room your opponent is getting his hands wrapped the same way." There was a quiet pause as the room reflected on the truth of those words. The athlete went silent and sat down with a reflective look of concern - the euphoria and confidence gone. Don't put your confidence in things that your opponent has too. You may be strong - so is your opponent. You may be fast - so is your opponent. You may be confident - so is your opponent. Put your faith in the things that you can build to a degree that others don't possess at your level - the things that training can create that separate you from others - your technique, tactics and preparation.

You've got five grappling limbs –
use them all: we think of ourselves as four limbed creatures, but in grappling your head can be used to push and pull an opponent just like your arms and legs - your goal is to maximize and integrate your use of all five. Grappling is all about connection to your opponent so that you can exert whatever forces you have upon him. Your limbs are the spearhead of that connection. That image of simultaneous and automatic use of all five limbs is what you must strive for as you grapple. Your torso is your engine, but your five limbs are the transmission that enable you to apply that power to your opponent.

Two for the price of one –

the dual power of leg locks from bottom position: When an opponent is in your guard his legs are his base of support. If you attack his upper body with submission holds he still initially has his legs under him giving him a stable base from which to defend himself. When you attack the legs with submission holds something interesting happens. Now you are attacking two things at once - his leg as a submission target and his base of support. It is so much harder to defend a lock when you are unstable. This usually forces the opponent to change his posture to sitting or kneeling to gain a new stable posture from which to defend his legs - and this immediately renders him vulnerable to follow up positional attacks. By attacking the legs, you create an automatic double attack and a follow-on attack that is extremely difficult to deal with when done well and which keeps an opponent on the defensive. Make sure you can threaten your opponent's legs from bottom position - you'll get twice the bang for the buck.

The return:

Tomorrow night in Austin Texas, Gordon Ryan will step out on stage again in an exhibition match against talented UFC middleweight Philip Rowe. Mr. Ryan has been locked in the toughest fight of his career against a lingering and debilitating stomach illness that has over time taken over his ability to train and prepare professionally for matches, prompting a time away from the game in an attempt to get it under control. Most of his biggest matches and victories have been fought under the shadow of this vexing problem - a testament to his ability to shrug off difficulties and focus on the win, but in the last year it has gotten to a point where daily training has been severely disrupted. He wants to stay active during this time and so exhibition matches are a good means of doing so. The rule set is actually quite interesting - almost like sparring in the gym as the two athletes will try to amass as many submissions as possible in the fifteen minutes allowed. This allows a full-length match and incentivized both athletes to take submission risks as you can get a second or third chance if it backfires. Thanks as always to FloGrappling and WNO for putting on great shows with interesting rule sets so that athletes can showcase their skills in what has become the premier industry event outside of the ADCC World Championships. Oliver Taza LBCA and Damien Anderson will be stepping on stage against very talented opponents among many top-level Jiu jitsu stars on this great card!

The pressure of the first mistake:
Gordon had a fascinating exhibition match last night in Austin Texas against talented MMA star Philip Rowe. Since it was an exhibition match there was not winner or loser - it was designed to give an interesting spectacle to fans who haven't seen Mr. Ryan onstage since his stomach issues deteriorated. The rule set allowed for as many submissions as possible in a given time (in this case fifteen minutes) so it had the feeling of a gym sparring session. This has a very positive effect in some ways because you get a second chance if you make a mistake and get caught in a submission hold - you just tap and start again. It's important to understand that in championship matches the outcome is usually decided by

WHOEVER MAKES THE FIRST MISTAKE OR WHOEVER MAKES THE LEAST MISTAKES. This is what makes championship matches so nerve wracking - mistakes are severely punished. The result is that athletes play a very conservative game built mostly around AVOIDING ERRORS rather than taking exciting risks. When athletes are given multiple chances to atone for an error they can open up a lot more and take risks. Last night's match reflected this with both men going for a full range of moves some of which they probably wouldn't ordinarily use in a high stakes match. To be sure I believe there is no substitute for conventional rule sets for championship matches - the need to avoid making errors and to capitalize on an opponent's errors is what creates the intense drama of big matches, but I do like the more laid back multiple chance rule set for exhibition matches where there is a bigger than usual discrepancy in skill level - it seemed to work well last night and could provide a fascinating alternative for spectators.

Traps:

If you face an opponent in a fiercely combative stance and posture you leave him nothing to work with and many opponents will be very reticent about engaging with you - leading to long bouts of passive inactivity. Sometimes you do better by deliberately leaving openings that will entice an opponent to enter. Lifting an elbow may entice an under hook, leaving a foot out unguarded may entice a leg lock attempt. Remember that the first line of defense is MENTAL - awareness of the threat. If you are not only aware of the danger but knowingly creating it yourself then it is extremely unlike an opponent will be able to exploit it before you spring the trap on him. As such, it's actually a fairly safe way to play despite the appearance of danger. This approach will often create engagement where it would otherwise not occur with a nervous opponent and it will be the best kind of engagement - engagement on your terms.

Footsweeps:

I think we all have moves that our favorites because they are high percentage and very effective for us - and moves that are favorites because they have an intrinsic cool or wow factor. For me, that was always foot sweeps. No other technique in all of combat sports conveys the effortless effect of total magic trick domination as a well applied foot sweep. In an instant you can drop or stumble an opponent seemingly with no effort, very little movement and low risk. The key is always to catch an unweighted foot. This means it requires timing and sensitivity to an opponent's footwork. As such it can be frustrating when you first try as you usually fail to catch the foot in a state of weightlessness. Foot sweeps are a move that either works brilliantly or not at all - there is no middle ground. So, have some patience when you start learning. It won't come overnight. However, the potential rewards to the patient student are immense. You will have a weapon that can drop an opponent in an instant or stumble them into a secondary technique. Usually footsweeps are applied with both athletes in the standing position, but be are they are equally effective when you're sitting and opponent is standing. Learn to catch that unweighted foot and you can make the mat into an ice-skating rink where everyone slips and falls in front of you!

Not every day in the gym will be a good one.
In fact, there will often be periods of weeks and even months where you feel like you're making no progress at all. There'll be days you swear you're going backwards. Disappointment and frustration occur more often than success in a tough room. Hang in there. Understand that everyone around you is progressing at a similar rate to you. Just as swimmers in a river current are carried at similar speeds by the river itself and so don't see much reward for all their attempts at swimming; so too the room rises and makes everyone in it feel like their effort doesn't make a difference. It does. You'll have a day every so often where you get to see the fruits of your work. That's how the game works. Long periods of tough work with apparently little progress and a few golden days randomly interspersed among them that reveal how far you've come. It's true that rates of improvement vary over time. It's true that some people can make faster progress than others. It's true that a change in training program can affect rates of progress - but I've never seen a case where someone trained regularly and sincerely and made NO progress. Rate of progress is important, but if your goals are long term, it doesn't matter too much whether you get to those goals a little sooner or a little later. Remember always that whatever doubts are inside your mind about your progress - the only way you won't improve at all over time is to stop showing up.

When you control the head...
An old clinch in grappling is that if you control the whole body. There is a LOT of truth to this. Learning to exploit the value of this insight is a big part of your progress in Jiu jitsu. It has many manifestations. One of the most important for grappling is the use

of the triangle not in its usual sense as a stranglehold, but rather as a means of immobilizing the head so that joint locks become more powerful. A fine example of this is Kimura. It can be very difficult to finish a Kimura when your opponent's head is free to move around. When you begin in a triangle that immobilizes the head and THEN apply a Kimura the results can be devastating. The same goes for armbars, even American locks and wrist locks. Much of the defense to these moves involves a preliminary movement of the head - when that is taken away the locks become far more difficult to escape and more devastating in their effects. Next time your triangle isn't working so we'll as a strangle - use it to attack with joint locks - I'm sure you'll be impressed with the results!

Never underestimate what a simple change of angle and level can do to improve your attack:
At any given moment of a match your opponent is making calculations and predictions and what you can and can't do based on his observations of your body positioning. He will position himself appropriately based on the beliefs he forms as a result of those observations. All this happens very quickly and changes very quickly as the match unfolds second by second. If you attack from where you currently are you will run directly into the positional roadblocks a good opponent will have put in front of you and get stopped or worse, countered. You need to change angle and level first so that you attack from a direction that your opponent has not blocked and press the attack before he can adapt his positioning to stop the new threat. Level changing in Jiu jitsu has many faces. Next time you want to press the action - don't just attack from where you are - change the level of the relevant part of your body (usually hips

and head) and angle and THEN attack - you'll get a lot more success that way.

The greatest positions in Jiu jitsu -

mount and rear mount: The game of Jiu jitsu rewards the mount and rear mount with more points than any other positional moves. I fact they score twice as much as takedowns, sweeps, knee on stomach and even outscore guard passing. As much as possible you should seek to get to these high reward positions. It's a fascinating question which is the better of the two. I generally put a premium on back over mount in grappling but slightly favor the mount in fighting when striking is involved. The real point is not however, which is better, but rather, how will you move smoothly from one to the other. Both positions involve the use of your legs wrapped around your opponent's hips or torso to exert control. WHENEVER AN OPPONENT TURNS OUT OF ONE POSITION HE WILL OFFER OPPORTUNITY TO TRANSITION TO THE OTHER. Learning to take advantage of this transition from mount to rear mount and rear mount to mount is key to your development in utilizing these devastating positions to maximum advantage. Understand that when an opponent goes to turn you want to HELP them by opening a little space with your legs. Jiu jitsu rewards these two positions more than any other - make sure you learn to move between them to reap those rewards to the greatest degree possible!

Rising up from bottom position:

Too often we have a mindset in Jiu jitsu that once we start in bottom position we have to stay there until we sweep or submit the opponent. This is unfortunate. Just because you start in bottom position doesn't mean you have to stay there. There are MANY occasions in sparring and competition where sufficient space develops between you and your opponent which will allow you to come up from bottom into takedowns (as opposed to conventional sweeps) and scrimmage for points in the ensuing scrambles you create - either reversing position or taking the opponents back as he tries to scramble away from the takedown. This mindset of staying down only when you are forced to stay down creates real pressure from bottom position and forces the top player to engage much more actively - this in turn makes conventional sweeps and submissions much easier, so ironically, by adding a little more wrestling into your game, your submission percentages often increase. Next time your opponent backs away from the sweeps and submissions you are using from guard position - rise up into takedowns - you will be pleasantly surprised how often this can get the score that was eluding you when an opponent is disengaging.

Adjustments:

submission holds are an all of nothing affair. A submission hold that was 99% perfect allows a skilled opponent to escape through that 1% error. A submission hold that was 99% perfect that failed scores nothing LEARNING TO TAKE A MOVE FROM 95% PERFECT TO 100% PERFECT IS ONE OF THE GREAT KEYS TO YOUR PROGRESS. Most submissions begin with an entry that is far from perfect, but good enough to hold an opponent in place long enough for a PERIOD OF ADJUSTMENT that transforms the move into one capable of actually finishing a tough opponent. Learning to ADJUST UNDER PRESSURE is the mark of the submission expert - and it must become part of your game. Submissions START with entry - but they FINISH with adjustment. Take the time to adjust and convert them from decent to good and from good to great - this is the way of the submission's expert.

Leverage and the spine:
The spine is the longest lever in the human body. It can be used as a great benefit in countless moves and situations - and it can be used AGAINST you in just as many. If you can control both ends of the lever - your opponent's hips and head - you will have gained a very significant mechanical advantage over your opponent. Control of both ends of the spine like this almost guarantees the guard pass. Controlling one end of the lever is good - controlling both ends is great. Look for this whenever you can - it doesn't always come easy, but when it does, you will be unstoppable.

Distance control:
One of the most important aspects of guard play is CONTROLLING THE DISTANCE BETWEEN YOU AND YOUR OPPONENT. If your opponent is move to move towards and away from you at will - he gets to choose when and how you engage - that's a big advantage for the top player. It's important you take those luxuries away from him and bestow them on yourself. Controlling distance without a Gi

can be a challenge as you don't have the Gi collar to help you. I generally find the best all round method is ashi garami. Your knee positioned in front of him makes it difficult and risky for an opponent to push towards you and also difficult to back away as you have a leg positioned behind him as well. As soon as you control distance it's time to attack the opponents balance - and then attack with sweeps and submissions. Start with grip into distance control, then off balancing, then the real attack. Multi-tiered approaches like this are what will make your guard a formidable weapon for any opponent.

Bad position?

Stance first - escape second: We all know that when you get caught in a bad position in Jiu jitsu the onus is on us to escape. Escape takes time however; and in that time, a good opponent will use that position to attack us with submissions. Therefore, your first responsibility in bad position is not escape, but rather, STANCE. You must adopt an appropriate defensive stance that reduces the possibility of an opponent submitting you and which facilitates your eventual escape. Initial Failures in defensive stance make it almost impossible to employ the escapes you know and make it much more likely you'll be tapping rather than escaping. When caught in a bad position start by getting your hands, elbows and knees inside your opponent's hands, elbows and hips to the greatest degree that you can. Off balancing an opponent with bridging, bumping and kipping helps this a lot. Once your arms and legs are inside your opponents you will find escape is considerably easier and there is a lot less danger of getting submitted. Next time you're in a bad position -

start with recovering your defensive stance - only then will the escapes you've been working on prove effective.

Your mind may be your most powerful weapon –
but your legs are a close second: The entire philosophy of Jiu jitsu bottom game is based on the idea that BOTTOM POSITION IS ONLY DISADVANTAGEOUS IF YOU CAN'T USE YOUR LEGS TO GRAPPLE YOUR OPPONENT. The whole game from bottom is to keep your legs between you and your opponent and to use them as your primary weapon. Here I work with a classic tripod sweep - a fine example of using the legs to engage an opponent standing over you. Remember that even though your legs are the power source behind the guard, it is your FEET that connect that power to an opponent - so make your feet grip your opponent with the same dexterity as your hands. This is a skill that takes time to develop but will be a key element in making your legs the basis of your bottom game.

The magic of half guard:
Every Jiu jitsu athlete has a responsibility to excel in bottom position. If you can't work effectively from bottom position you'll never reliably defeat bigger opponents or opponents with better takedowns than you. The question becomes - which bottom position will be your workhorse? There are many choices, each with their strengths and weaknesses. There is a lot to be said for half guard as your bottom game foundation. Any time you work from half guard

with a good under hook you are immediately half way to your opponent's back and halfway to a single leg takedown. This is a huge potential advantage if you know how to use it. It gives you a definite initial advantage that can be made to work strongly in your favor. Your opponent has to compensate for this with grip and body position and you can play off this compensation and play a very simple but strong sweeping game. In order to shut down that sweeping game he will make himself vulnerable to the initial threat of back exposure and single leg takedowns that he was trying to compensate for! The whole time there is so much body contact that it's extremely difficult for your opponent to simply disengage - it can be a real problem for even very tough opponents. If you struggle to be effective from bottom position and are looking for a sense of direction that will work well in almost every context - Gi or no Gi, grappling or MMA, try half guard. The whole method of Jiu jitsu bus to gain prior advantage before attacking, and half guard bottom can definitely offer that if you know the right starting positions.

Keep your hands up!!!!
Every time you go to watch a boxing match there is some guy screaming at every fighter to keep their hands up. Of course, there is an undeniable validity to the old cliché even if it is an over simplification with many exceptions. It expresses the need for defensive awareness and soundness - to protect the most vulnerable part of the body in a boxing match - the chin. Similarly, in Jiu jitsu. We also, also need to keep our hands up at times, but not to defend the chin since there is no striking - it is to defend the NECK - not from the danger of a punch, but from the danger of a STRANGLE. Make sure always to use your hand OPPOSITE the entering strangle

hand if he is behind you and SAME side if he is in front of you. Keeping your hands up in these circumstances can stop small problems becoming big problems. As in boxing, don't overdo the "hands up" philosophy - but just as in boxing, don't under do it either - defensive soundness is the core of sensible Jiu jitsu and early neck protection is a big part of that.

If you can SEE your opponent's back - you can TAKE his back:
The back is a big part of the surface area of our body - that makes it a big target. Not only is it a BIG target - it's a LUCRATIVE target. Nothing else scores more points and nothing else gives more high percentage and safe position to submit your opponent. As such, there will be MANY opportunities to take an opponent's back in any extended engagement. In fact, there will be MANY MORE THAN YOU REALIZE AND THAT YOU TAKE ADVANTAGE OF. You have to train your mind to see the opportunities before your body can make the movements to take advantage of them all. If you can see even a small percentage of your opponent's back for just a second or two - there is almost always a way to navigate your body to his back. Learning to believe and take advantage of this insight is one of the greatest ways to speed your progress and success rate in Jiu jitsu. What the eyes see, the rest of your body can capture - next time you see a flash of your opponent's back - be ready to take the prize!

Outstanding!!

The ADCC North American trials have been on this weekend with many amazing performances from the athletes across all weight divisions. Among those great performances were two that have a remarkable element that pertains to many of my readers. I teach my instructional videos at BJJ Fanatics in Boston and two of the main demonstrations partners I work with are Placido Santos and Giancarlo Bodoni, both of who regularly appear in my videos. Over the years they have diligently worked on the material we cover and often travel long distances for extended periods of time to come to train with us. Giancarlo recently moved to Austin to train with us full time. That dedication paid off with both men having outstanding performances in the trials. Giancarlo won Gold in his division and punched his ticket to the biggest event in grappling - the next ADCC world championships next year. He won against the biggest field in trials history over two grueling days. Placido came out guns blazing on the first two with a spectacular run of submissions - both men had a very high submission rate. It's amazing to see the transformation that new knowledge and new ways of thinking can have on a self-motivated and dedicated student who puts in the work necessary to transform knowledge into skill. I am so proud of their performances and the way they showed how long-distance learning can have a powerful effect on your Jiu jitsu game. Thank you also to Gordon Ryan who did a very fine job of cornering both athletes - his experience in ADCC competition is such a help. Thank you also to BJJ Fanatics Bernardo Faria and Michael Zenga, who came to watch their two most famous employees put on the best performance of their lives this weekend! Well done Giancarlo and Placido!

Push and pull:
Every grappling exchange has a beginning based around establishing grip. Once that is attained it's natural to want to go straight into your attacks. That can certainly work, but often you are well advised to start with a brief period of PUSH and PULL that creates the possibility of ACTION and REACTION. Learning to play constructively with those reactions to your pushing and pulling is one of the biggest steps you can make in your grappling journey. Next time you lock up with your partner, don't rush to your moves. Start with a brief period of push and pull using both arms and legs and try to feed of the reactions you get and use those reactions to enter your moves. Adding that intermediary step of push and pull - no matter how brief - will add a whole new dimension of attacking skills to your game.

Most targets get more difficult to attack as the match goes on -
the back is the exception to the rule: I'm sure you have all had the experience of trying to attack a submission hold towards the end of a match and found out the hard way that the inevitable sweat and overall slipperiness makes it very difficult to control and finish many of the major submissions. Most arm locks and leg locks become more difficult as sweat and slipperiness increase. Interestingly however, getting to an opponent's back is barely affected by increases in slipperiness and arguably may even be EASIER. Many transitions to the back are helped by increased slipperiness rather than hindered. Sliding your strangle arm into position also becomes easier with less friction. Holding the back for extended periods of time can be a little more difficult, but nothing

that wrist control, good head position and a tight body triangle can't take care of. Next time your favorite submissions are failing in slippery conditions - focus on transitions to the back - they will make your work easier rather than harder.

Beginners in Jiu jitsu ignore their opponent's grips and entanglements
 because they don't understand the dangers they lead to. As they learn and develop expertise they come to see the danger and start to break grips as soon as they become a threat. But the very best athletes go back to the start and ignore grips - this time not from ignorance, but from the knowledge that if you reach a high enough level you can let an opponent take any grip he likes and use it as the opening to your own attacks. The opponents grip becomes a shortcut to your own offense.

Starting with an advantage:
Imagine if you were practicing takedowns with an opponent your own size and skill level and he told you he would let you start in a full single position - no hand fighting, no level changing, no shooting needed - you get the position for free. I'm sure you'd be pretty happy about that because it would take out some of the most difficult elements of takedowns and let you start with half the task already completed. Well, that's pretty much what happens when you start in a good half guard position with an under hook. You essentially start in a single leg position. No need for all the difficulties of hand

fighting, level changing and shooting - you're already in on the leg and ready to go - that's a big advantage! You could also say similar things about getting to an opponent's back - you're half way there also - the only thing between you and your opponent's back is his over hook/whizzer. Beat that and the back is yours. Next time you're working from half guard with an under hook - remind yourself that you begin half way to a single leg and/or the back and take heart that by getting to half guard you've gotten half way to two great situations before the action has even begun!

Breaking posture:
If there is one word of advice I could give students who are trying to attack an opponent with positional moves or submission a greater chance of success it would be this - START EVERY ATTACK WITH AN ATTACK ON YOUR OPPONENTS POSTURE. Your opponent's defense is only as strong as the integrity of his posture. Break his posture and it will be relatively easy to break whatever else you want.

When you've got a choice...
Very often the scenario we find ourselves in presents a choice in finishing options. A classic example is triangle and arm bar. WHENEVER YOU HAVE ONE OF THESE OPTIONS - YOU ALMOST ALWAYS HAVE THE OTHER AS WELL. As a general rule - I always urge my students to take the triangle option over the arm bar option all other things being equal. Of course, there will be

exceptions to this general rule. For example, if your opponents have very broad shoulders and you have short legs, it's probably best to stick with the arm bar option. However, the triangle offers the option of both strangle and multiple joint locks at the same time - all backed up by a much tighter control of the head than an arm bar due to the figure four lock. The arm bar on the other hand offers only a single joint lock and much looser head control. So, given the choice, triangle will be my preference. Next time your attacking arm bars and the finish isn't coming quickly - perhaps try a switch to a triangle and see if you can use some of the inherent advantages to help your cause.

Posture:

For every task in grappling there is an ideal posture that maximizes your effectiveness and minimizes your workload. These postures vary wildly depending upon the task at hand. Sometimes it will require upright posture. Sometimes a sprinters posture. Sometimes a hunched posture. The list has as many variations as there are tasks. What works well in one scenario will perform poorly in another. Your task is to understand which posture is suited to which task and then stay as true to that ideal posture as you can until the task is completed and you switch to the next task and a new posture. If you want to know what is the ideal posture for a given task - try the task - you will quickly find that a certain posture makes it seem easier and any deviation from that posture is progressively punished depending on how far you stray from the ideal. At the end of the day this sport of ours is ultimately a game of MOVEMENT and POSTURE before anything else. The deeper your knowledge of these two elements and how they pertain to the goals of the game, the further you will go with everything else in the sport.

Taking the power out of your opponent's side pins – getting under hooks: It's never any fun getting pinned by a good top player. Not only is it hard to move - sometimes it's hard even to breath - and a skilled opponent is constantly threatening to convert the pin into a submission hold. You can take way much of the power of your opponent's side pins by consistently pommeling your arms under and inside his into under hooks. This greatly undermines his connection to your torso and allows you turn onto your side rather than flat on your back. This immediately takes pressure off the diaphragm and helps you breath more easily. It also allows much easier movement towards guard position and/or getting up to your knees to escape the pin. In addition, it greatly reduces the immediate danger of most of the standard submissions from this position. It doesn't take much to get that under hook in, but the rewards are great. Next time you're suffering under a smothering side pin, rather than just try to bulldoze your way out, work to get both your arms under his first. Then get on to your side and you'll find that everything from breathing to movement to escapes become significantly easier and less risky.

The heavier your opponent's chest becomes – the lighter his legs become: Jiu jitsu is a game of weight distribution. Sometimes it can very intimidating to feel an opponent putting all his weight on to one part of your body. Remember however, that the more an opponent uses his weight to crush one part of you, the more he must lighten some other part of his body. If you remember this you can use this to your advantage. Next time your suffering under weight distribution - be confident that the heavier the distribution in one area - THE LIGHTER IN ANOTHER - and navigate a course to take advantage of that the light zone (hint: it's almost always some form of elbow escape or bridge escape) and turn a hard time into a success.

It doesn't seem like a big difference...

One of the hardest truths to convince a beginner in Jiu jitsu of is that there is a world of difference between being FLAT ON YOUR BACK underneath an opponent, as opposed to BEING ON YOUR SIDE. To the untrained eye they look pretty much the same. You are lying down underneath an opponent in both cases after all. In fact, the difference will determine how effective you will be from bottom position. When you're on your side you can bear an opponent's weight much more easily. You can move side to side far more readily. You can prop yourself up to an elbow or turn easily up to your knees, or reach out with your legs and catch an opponent's leg. You can create an action/reaction sequence by turning from one side to another. In short - you don't bear weight directly and you can move much more readily. Understanding the importance of this fundamental insight and making it part of your daily training is absolutely critical to your progress in most Bottom positions, particularly those your opponent is threatening to pass your legs. Next time you're suffering under an opponent's weight - turn to your side (almost always towards your opponent) and you'll feel an immediate easing of pressure and a newfound ability to move with effect.

When working from guard position –
actively seek to get your opponent's hands on the floor: It can be difficult learning to grapple effectively from bottom position when you begin Jiu jitsu. It always seems that the top player has everything in his favor and that you begin with a massive disadvantage. In time you'll see that this is not the case, but early on it's natural to feel that way. One piece of advice that can greatly help speed up your development in this area is this - LOOK TO GET YOUR OPPONENTS HANDS TO THE FLOOR WHENEVER POSSIBLE. It's not always possible nor necessary to get his hands to the floor to attack from guard, but it does create a very effective line of attack that will give you direction and focus when starting out. When you off balance an opponent and force his hands to the mat against his will, he cannot present any passing danger to you not use his hands defensively against whatever follow up attacks you employ until he recovers his balance and stance. In that time, you will have an open door through which to attack. In addition, hands on floor opens his whole body to attacks. You can attack lower body or upper body with equal efficacy. Next time you're feeling frustrated with your bottom game start by getting his hands to the mat and THEN attacking with your favorite moves. You may be pleasantly surprised that opponents who were previously shutting you down are suddenly a little easier to attack with success.

The first guard you learn:
When I began Jiu jitsu it was standard practice to begin the study of guard position with closed guard. There is a lot of wisdom to this. Closed guard has good value as a self-defense position and that was an important consideration at that time as Jiu jitsu was closely linked to early MMA and fighting in general. As my experience as a coach grew I came to question whether closed guard was always the best choice for the first guard position for everyone. I always noticed that most beginner students had an easier time becoming effective from half guard than they did from full guard. Moreover, closed guard tended to favor the longer legged athletes over short limbed athletes. Half guard seemed to work equally for all body types. In addition, half guard integrated extremely well with pin escapes and allowed students to easily transition from a defensive elbow escape directly into half guard offense. Ultimately, I came to believe that there is no one guard that ought to be learned before all others. Like everything in life, different people will gravitate towards what they are best suited for. I therefore don't dictate what kind of guard comes first but rather show a variety of fundamental guards (nothing crazy at beginner level) and let people decide whether they prefer guards based on outside control such as closed guard, or inside control such as butterfly guard or a mix of both, such as half guard. In the end, you're going to have to learn all the various guard positions to some degree, which one you learn first doesn't seem to affect long term development that much, so start with the ones best suited to your body. The main thing is that you gain COMPETENCE THAT LEADS TO CONFIDENCE in your bottom game as early as possible that you overcome quickly our natural trepidation about fighting from underneath tough opponents.

Approach as every match and every scenario within a match as A PROBLEM TO BE SOLVED
rather than as an ORDEAL TO BE OVERCOME. Your problem-solving ability is among the most important elements in attaining victory - arguably the most important. Courage, tenacity, will, strength, resilience and all the other attributes and virtues are wonderful things - but when there is a door to be opened, hammering, kicking, smashing and ramming may do it, nothing does it so well and so easily as a key. Your ability to apply knowledge and figure out solutions is the key to every lock. Put your emphasis on that above all else.

Sitting on the sidelines:
There will always be times injury takes you off the mat. Whenever that occurs I always encourage students to come in and watch. Part of the motivation is to keep their spirits up, but far more important is the need to keep their progress going even when you can't physically participate. Never forget that every physical action in Jiu jitsu begins with a mental decision to act that way. You can use this insight to help your progress when you can't physically perform the moves. Watch matches from the sideline - but don't watch for ENTERTAINMENT by simply seeing who wins and who loses. Watch to LEARN and IMPROVE by MENTALLY PARTICIPATING IN THE MATCHES YOU WATCH. Put yourself in the place of the two athletes, sometimes the offensive player and sometimes the defensive player. Don't FOLLOW the action with your eyes, PREDICT and JUDGE the action with your MIND. This

is the best and most important participation you can engage in when your body can't engage. When the body can't engage - THE MIND STILL CAN - and that mental engagement will allow noticeable improvement when you return. Never forget that physical action begins with mental decisions and use this to your advantage next time you can't physically train.

Stacking the odds in your favor:
Jiu jitsu is never easy, any time your engaged against someone your own size and skill level every match will be a tough trial. Nonetheless there are some things you can do to make things a little easier. You can see here that from bottom position I have focused on. First, distance control. I have applied an Ashi Garami that puts a knee in front of my opponent to prevent him easily moving forward and a knee behind him to prevent him easily moving backwards. In addition, I have knocked his hands to the floor. This immediately means he is carrying most of his own weight on his hands. If he is carrying his own weight, then I don't have to. As such my work load has decreased significantly. In addition, his lower body becomes lighter as he carried weight on his hands making leg submissions easier to enter into. Perhaps most importantly, if his hands are on the floor then they aren't on me - as such it will be very difficult for an opponent to engage in any guard passing until he has corrected his posture, giving me uncontested attacks until he corrects himself. Thirdly, I have an advantageous angle where I have positioned myself outside his elbows and thus can attack from the side rather than frontally. Seen in this light you can see that attacks that begin

with a deliberate attempt to stack the odds in your favor are far more likely to succeed than those where you simply make up your mind to use a certain move and go straight to it. Understanding what undermines an opponent's defenses is critical to developing your ability to beat skilled opponents. Just as important as learning moves are the precursors to those moves so that you can create an unfair advantage in your favor before you even attempt them.

Interfering hands:
It always seems every time you go to hit a move from guard your opponent's hands are always working to dislodge the grip of your legs and shit down your sweep attempt. Whenever this happens - attack his balance. If he doesn't use his hands for balance he'll fall. If he does release and use his hands for balance and base - he won't be able to interfere with your guard and you can attack again. Don't accept those disruptive hands. If he puts hands on your legs - knock him off balance immediately and play off his reaction to it.

Extraordinary degrees of resistance:
I'm sure you've had the experience of sparring with a physically imposing opponent and you find that your moves, even your favorites, don't seem to work against this level of physicality. You will often find that extraordinary levels of flexibility or strength can

make your moves feel inadequate. When you feel this this - take heart - you're not this first to feel this way!! Some general words of advice. If your opponent has rubber joints that seem immune to your favorite locks - focus on strangles. If you can't strangle successfully with your arms due to freakish hand strength or jaw blocking of opponents - strangle with your legs. If your opponent has the strength to bench press you out of any form of top control - focus on getting behind him. If your opponent has a Gumby like guard that appears impossible to pass into top position - focus on taking the back instead. There is always a shift in tactics that can make up for physical freaks that frustrate your favorite lines of attack. Don't get intimidated by unusual physical attributes - get inspired - inspired to try a new approach that shows how tactics and technique prevail or physicality.

If you want to move people –

get under their center of gravity: it is never easy to move someone who doesn't want to be moved. It's even worse when they are bigger and heavier than you. Probably the most reliable means of doing so is to get UNDER THEIR CENTER OF GRAVITY. If you can do this it becomes MUCH easier to lift and move your opponent. From bottom position you have to make your body compact and get down low. You will need some form of effective connection to your opponent - it's no good getting under someone if you can't stay there long enough to complete a move. A good place to start playing around with this concept is bottom half guard. From there is relatively easy to burrow under an opponent if you can get an arm under theirs and around the waist. Once under their center of gravity you will find it quite easy to roll side to side and carry them with you - that's the location and feeling you want - like their center of gravity is floating over yours - once you can move an opponent you can sweep or throw him.

When one part of your body is in trouble -
other parts have to come to the rescue: The game of Jiu jitsu is all about isolating one part of an opponent's body and attacking it. Sometimes you will be on the wrong side of that methodology and find one part of your body has been isolated and about to be attacked. If you can react early enough then it's usually possible to simply pull the endangered limb free. However, if your opponent is doing a good job of restricting your movement you'll need a more sophisticated approach. Rather than desperately try to extract your isolated limb - look to use other parts of your body to protect it. Here I am being effectively pinned in side control and my left arm has been isolated by an under hook. I react by wedging my right knee at the pocket of my opponents right hip and right forearm at the pocket of the left hip. This immediately restricts my opponent's movement and makes it more difficult for him to transition into mount or move around to the other side of my body for upper body submission attacks. There is a sense in which I lost a battle on my left-hand side and so I must win on the right-hand side in order to prevent further loss. Once this barrier of elbow and knee on the right side has been established, any movement by my opponent will create sufficient space to join knee and elbow together as a locked

frame and out the opponent back in guard where the isolated left arm won't be any use. Next time you're stuck and arm or leg isolated - use this line of thinking to first protect yourself and then work safely out of the position and back on the attack!

Defense into offense:

The moves of Jiu jitsu are divided evenly into offense and defense. A perfect defensive game would make you undefeatable. A perfect offensive game would make you capable of defeating anyone. As a general rule it's best to begin your study with a bias towards defense, since the most common scenario for anyone starting out in the sport is to be overwhelmed by their more knowledgeable and experienced classmates. Somewhere along the road of your development however, you must begin to synthesize defense and offense. THE COMPLETION OF ALMOST EVERY DEFENSIVE MOVE IN JIU JITSU IS RICH IN ATTACKING OPPORTUNITY FOR THOSE WHO LOOK FOR IT. Here I have stopped an initial leg tackle down on the mat - the second the initial danger has passed it's time to switch gears from defense into offense. There are great positional opportunities here - go behinds to the back will always be foremost among them - and also submission opportunities - anything out of front head lock will be a great choice, but there are many others as well. Next time you've successfully stopped an opponent with your defense - don't be satisfied with stopping them - go immediately into counter offense. You will soon find that opponents are much easier to attack due to being somewhat out of position after their failed attack and you can make the synthesis of defense and offense work strongly in your favor.

Angle:

We all figure out how early on in our development that is hard to attack someone directly from the front - you immediately run into their strongest lines of defense - the hands and head. Most success comes from circumventing those major lines of defense. In grappling this is done in two major ways - LEVEL and ANGLE. You can go UNDER and AROUND your opponent's defenses much more easily that going THROUGH them. It's not easy to get advantageous angle on good opponents. Usually there has to be some form of distraction or misdirection first - but once you've got - it's a great momentary advantage that you must use immediately as it won't last forever. Understand that angular change doesn't have to be dramatic to be effective. Here in a drill I have gotten to perpendicular - that's great but difficult on a resisting opponent - you only need enough angle to slip outside head and hands - even a small angular advantage can yield good results. It's particularly important when working to pass guard on top of attack from guard on bottom. Next time you're working from either - don't make your first move TOWARDS you opponent but rather AROUND your opponent and see if you can get better success with your attacks as a result.

You always go out alone:
Jiu jitsu is an odd sport insofar as it is practiced as a group but when it's time to perform it's you and you alone who steps out in the mat. You can be surrounded by your friends, coaches and teammates but when your name is called it's only you that walks out. This dichotomy between the social aspect of group training and the inner loneliness of your solo performance is at the heart of your Jiu jitsu experience. It manifests itself in athletes in dramatic ways - some athletes excel in the gym and struggle on the stage. Others look ordinary in the gym and shine on stage. The main thing is to grasp the significance of the fact that ultimately you can be given all manner of advice, comfort and encouragement by everyone you know - but it's YOU and you like who will have to perform - so make sure you develop a game that suits YOU and that your game is an expression of who YOU are - not anyone else. Just as you can easily see when a person is not comfortable inside their own skin, you can easily see when an athlete is not comfortable with their own game or match persona. So, when it's time to build your game - yes, it's good to take advice and learn from the experience of others - but don't do so to the extent that your game is more an expression of someone else's Jiu jitsu than your own, because when your name is called they won't be coming out on the mat with you.

What is Jiu jitsu really about?
More than anything else Jiu Jitsu is about compensating for inequalities in physical attributes between different people. The day we are conceived we are thrown into the genetic lottery which will

determine our size, speed and many other physical attributes. The day we are born we are thrown into the hands of fate which will determine much of our development. By the time we are old enough to think we start to note that many or perhaps even most of the people around us have considerable physical advantages over us. So often everyone else seems faster, stronger, more flexible, heavier, taller, longer reach - the list goes on. It can reach into mental attributes as well. Our peers seem more confident, smarter, more aggressive etc. We are left looking at ourselves in the mirror as ungifted in comparison. JIU JITSU IS OUR ATTEMPT TO USE MECHANICS, TECHNIQUE AND TACTICS TO COMPENSATE FOR OUR PHYSICAL AND EVEN MENTAL SHORTCOMINGS. Leverage can make a weak person strong. Good position can make a strong person feel weak. Anticipation can make a slow person fast. Precise pinning can make a light person heavy. Good off balancing can make a heavy person light. Strangleholds can pacify even the most aggressive people. Success over time in training can make a coward brave and the timid confident. There are many things in life in which you have little choice. Jiu jitsu is a means by which you can make a stand and redefine who you are through study and training. In this sense the choice to study Jiu jitsu is your chance to overcome all those areas of your life in which you felt you had no choice and in which it seemed you were disadvantaged. I've seen many things in the course of my life but perhaps one of the most remarkable has been the degree to which the study of Jiu jitsu grips so many people from so many backgrounds with a passion and enthusiasm for participation and improvement that I don't see in most sports, where most involvement is simply as a spectator or as a game that is fun to play rather than as a way to change who they are.

Failure vs potential:
When we look at our performance in Jiu jitsu we tend to lump everything into two categories - success and failure. Moves either work or they don't - they succeed or fail. If you adopt this mindset there is little chance that you will make technical progress over time. The reason is simple - whenever we learn new moves it is almost certain that the vast majority of applications when we start out will fail. When we first learn a move our performance of it is usually (and understandably) poor. It takes time to build skill. It will take time for you to take a move from infancy to adulthood. A much better approach is to asses moves not by success or failure, but by potential. The best indicator of general potential is usually not from you, but comes from watching high level athletes performing the move in top level competition. If the move works repeatedly there then it's likely it will work at whatever level you are. Then start asking if it has specific potential for YOU. As yourself if it works for a wide array of body types and levels of athleticism. If it requires such extreme athletic abilities that only a handful of people can apply well, it may not have potential for you. Then start your personal journey with the move. Start small. Don't try it first with the toughest guy in your gym. Try it on lesser targets until you feel ready to move up. When you first try it, you will soon get a sense of whether the move feels natural to you. Even if it's not fully succeeding at first of you can feel POTENTIAL - perhaps you ALMOST get it to work a couple of times, that's a good sign that it's worth more work and time. In time a move that almost works can become a move works really well almost every time. Success or failure isn't the yardstick of new moves - potential is.

Your opponent can never cover all the potential targets:
In all combat sports the basic game is to be able to attack vulnerabilities in an opponent whilst defending your own. Sometimes opponents have excellent discipline with their stance and positioning so that it feels impossible to breach their defenses. Take heart - it may seem this way - but it's an illusion - there's ALWAYS an opening somewhere. The more an opponent focuses his attention on defending one piece of real estate, the more vulnerable he becomes at some other area. If he spreads his defenses over his whole body, he won't be able to stop a determined attack anywhere. That's the basic dilemma that must guide your target selection. This why is why two things are necessary for you to breach tough defenses. The first is a wide enough array of attacks to cover the whole body. This means you should have at least one strong attack for lower body, upper body and neck from front and back. The second thing you need is the ability to feint an attack in one area to draw his defenses into one zone whilst being able to redirect to another which is now undefended. Don't just choose your main attacks randomly. Make sure you have enough variety to cover the whole body from front and back and top to bottom; and on top of that, the ability to trick an opponent into believing that an attack is imminent in one place when in fact you will attack another target. When you have these two elements in your attack game, you will find that even tough defenses that used to shut you out can be breached.

In the midst of all defense are the seeds of offense:

It's natural when an opponent attacks you to focus only on saving yourself. Early in your development that's the best thing to do, but at some point, you have to see ANY TIME AN OPPONENT ATTACKS YOU HE MUST MAKE COMPROMISES WITH HIS DEFENSIVE INTEGRITY, HIS BALANCE, HIS STANCE AND HIS FOCUS. This means that an astute player will see his opponent's offense as a fine entry into his own offense. This kind of counter offense has significant advantages over conventional offense since it is performed against an opponent who is compromised physically by being over extended and mentally by being focused on attack rather than his defense. It can be difficult initially to make this mental shift. You will need to clearly identify points at which the attack has been neutralized and a turning point achieved where you can initiate your counter attack. I suggest you start this project with your current favorite submission since you have greater expertise here. Ask yourself what criteria would make it fail and make you abandon it. Then have an opponent attack you with it. Work to satisfy those criteria and as soon as you've done so - counterattack! Once you're comfortable with your favorite submissions, start expanding the project into others. Soon you will have an arsenal of counter attacks that will greatly increase the number of submission attempts you make per match.

The power of the triangle:
Oliver Taza had a fine win last night in the Emerald City Invitational grappling tournament last night. It featured EBI rules and had some great matches. In the finals he came up against talented former team mate Nick Ronan and it went to overtime. In an arm bar situation Mr. Taza made a transition to a side triangle - Yoko Sankaku - and took a fine submission win in addition to his other submission victories via his powerful leg lock game. The triangle is one of the very best upper body submissions and one you all must devote serious study to. Unfortunately, in Jiu jitsu when people talk of the triangle they usually only refer to one form of triangle - the front triangle - and mostly think of it as a weapon from guard. Interestingly in judo the side triangle is seen much more than the front triangle due to the fact that guard position is not as heavily emphasized as it is in Jiu jitsu and Turtle position is more heavily emphasized than it is in Jiu jitsu. There are five major forms of triangle and they can be done from many scenarios. Only when you see all the types of triangles and the many scenarios they can be employed from will you start to reach your potential with this great move.

A life of routine:
We talk about a routine life as though it's a bad thing - disparaging it as dull and boring and indicative of failed life choices. Let me be clear - almost all of our progress and achievement in life is founded upon the acquisition of skills, and skills are only acquired through the maintenance of a routine that gives you sufficient time and

repetition to let them develop. If you want progress in Jiu jitsu or any other aspect in life, you will need to establish a routine and everything else in your life will have to be arranged around that routine. That doesn't mean you have to condemn yourself to a dull life of boredom - but it does mean that you will have to avoid anything that interrupts the routine in a significant way. Routine isn't something to be disparaged - on the contrary - it is the source and wellspring of your greatest resource - skill - and if you wish to rise to the top of your domain it will be skills developed by adherence to that routine that allow you to do so.

Contrasts:

The game of Jiu jitsu requires us to work with extremes of physical tension from very high to very low. As a general rule, you want to keep your body tension as low as possible to get the job done and recognize that some jobs require a considerable amount of tension for short periods of time. So, for example, submission holds, guard passes, sweeps and takedowns will require short burst of massive physical tension and output when you go to complete them. Understand that you can only maintain that level of intensity for short bursts - don't stay above the redline too long and exhaust yourself. This game is characterized by LONG PERIODS OF RELATIVE CALM INTERSPERSED WITH SHORT BURSTS OF EXTREME EXERTION. If you break this pattern by being too relaxed all the time you won't have sufficient energy to finish moves and score. If you break it by maintaining tension too long you will exhaust yourself and lose to your own fatigue. Keep this behavioral pattern of tension and relaxation in mind as you train every day and you will last longer and break through more.

When you've got one – you've often got another: We tend to think in terms of what's right in front of us and get myopic about what's further ahead. While it's certainly good to be focused on the here and now and try hard to finish the task in front of us - we have to be realistic also - and the reality is that when you're matched against someone your own size and skill level most of your initial attacks will fail due to strong resistance. As such, it's very important you be able to look past the current attack and see the next possibility. A really good place for you to start training your mind and body this way is with the arm bar Juji Gatame. Why? Because Juji Gatame cuts across the upper middle of the human body at an angle that gives you direct access to triangles and Ashi Garami leg locks as well as the original arm bar - any time you have the position for Juji Gatame you can thread yourself easily into variations of triangles and Ashi Garami leg locks (and if you're creative you can find other alternatives as well). Spend some time playing around in the Juji Gatame position - thread your legs into different types of triangles. Reach down for a leg and drop into leg locks - pretty soon you will find yourself habitually looking beyond the first attack into follow up attacks - and that's a big part of what will get your beating better opponents in the future.

If you could have only one finishing hold for the rest of your life –

what would it be? For me it would be the rear strangle without question. It is the most reliable finishing hold of all. It does matter how mentally tough the opponent is - a strangle will incapacitate him and end the match. If an initial attempt should fail - you still have the position and can keep trying until you succeed. The position you use it from puts you in a situation where you can attack at will as many times as it takes to get the breakthrough. It requires no special physical characteristics and can definitely be used by smaller people to defeat bigger and stronger people. It works for short people, tall people, thin people and thick people. It works equally well in both grappling and fighting. It is the perfect embodiment of the Jiu jitsu philosophy of position before submission. With this in mind - you owe it to yourself to develop a PERFECT rear strangle. Study it and perfect it. If there is ONE finishing move in the sport that is truly worth perfecting it is this one. Don't settle for a decent rear strangle - make yours the very best you can. Life is full of sham products that aren't worth the time and effort we put into acquiring them - the rear strangle is a true gem that is worth every second of time and ounce of sweat you put into its development, refinement and perfection - don't settle for anything less.

Athleticism:

I think it's fair to say most people in Jiu jitsu have a feeling that everyone else in the room is a better athlete than they are. Yet when you ask them what they mean by this they point to a list of physical attributes - speed, flexibility, endurance etc. and say that most people possess these in greater amounts than they do and this makes them inherently better athletes or possessed of greater athletic potential. In fact, the single biggest contributor to your athletic potential at any given second in a match is not genetic - it's learned - it is your STANCE. Every task in the sport has a stance or posture that determines how efficiently you will perform that task. I don't care how good someone's genetic athleticism is (however you understand that) - IF THEY ARE IN A POOR STANCE FOR A GIVEN TASK, THEY WILL STRUGGLE TO PERFORM THAT TASK. The converse is also true. NO MATTER HOW POOR YOUR PERCEIVED ATHLETIC POTENTIAL IS, IF YOU ARE IN A GOOD STANCE TO PERFORM A GIVEN TASK, YOU WILL MAKE IT LOOK EASY. Your objective athletic potential is heavily dependent on factors outside your control, but plays much less of a role than many people think in the here and now of a match. Much more important is MAXIMIZING WHATEVER ATHLETIC POTENTIAL YOU HAVE BY TAKING A STANCE THAT MAXIMIZES PERFORMANCE OF THE TASK IMMEDIATELY IN FRONT OF YOU. Don't worry too much about whatever objective athleticism fate gave you. Focus instead on the athletic potential you give YOURSELF by adopting a strong and appropriate stance for the task in front of you.

Distance control:

Controlling the distance between you and your opponent is among the most important and fundamental skills in all combat sports. It is done very differently from one combat sports to another, depending upon the rules and objectives. In Jiu jitsu it is done primarily through grip, although movement is also very important. From guard bottom position distance control is usually achieved with the collar grip, but in no Gi Jiu jitsu you will need other methods. Closed guard is the one we usually start with when beginning Jiu jitsu. Ultimately distance control is the ability to control an opponent's ability towards and away from you. Locking your legs around your opponent is a good way to do this. However, you'll need good methods from open guard too. My favorite is always Ashi Garami. It fulfills the most important requirement of distance control - it controls movement forward and backwards because you have one leg behind an opponent's leg (controls movement backwards) and one in front (controls movement forwards). In addition, it allows you to attack your opponent's balance and threaten leg locks at all times. In order to have an effective bottom guard game you'll need an effective means of controlling distance. It doesn't matter which you choose, Ashi Garami, De la Riva, reverse De la Riva or any other method, just so long as you have at least one good form of connection that controls movement forward and back and sets up attacks.

Your game reveals who you are:
In daily life you reveal much about yourself by choices you make - you reveal superficial aspects of who you are by where you live, where you work, what car you drive, who you spend time with, how you dress. You reveal deeper aspects by life goals, your most cherished beliefs etc. Jiu jitsu is the same. The kind of game you play, the moves you favor, the manner in which you employ those moves, the level you aspire to and the time and effort you invest in training all spell out much of who you are as a person. The three most important things that influence your Jiu jitsu development are your body, your personality and your teachers. Who you are on the mat will be a reflection of these three factors. Two athletes can have the same favorite moves but have two totally different personalities, say one is brash and confident and the other shy and withdrawn - they may favor the same moves but their differences in personality will make them employ those moves very differently. Two athletes can have similar bodies and personalities but if they come from very different teaching lineages they will usually have very different games. Your body and personality are yours - they are your internal influences. Your teachers are an external influence. When you first begin the external influence is more important because you know nothing and need direction; but as time passes and you mature the internal influences naturally start to take precedence and your game becomes an authentic expression of who you are physically and mentally.

Wasted minutes:

A minute or two of your time doesn't seem like much - unless you're in a six-minute Jiu jitsu match. In matches less than ten minutes a minute or two is a big deal. It's not enough to simply be able to perform moves - you must be able to do so in a timely manner. A good example is sitting inside an opponent's closed guard. Time spent inside an opponent's closed guard is wasted time. You can score anything there and you can't attack with any high percentage submissions from there - but your opponent certainly can! As such you want to spend as little time as possible inside an opponent's closed guard - nothing good happens inside there. I find that the most reliable method is to stand up and open the closed guard. It's not the only way of doing it but it's the best one for smaller and shorter athletes to realistically open a bigger and taller opponent's closed guard. It can be done in a short time period and allows you to minimize time spent in a position where you can't score but the other guy can - never where you want to be in this game. Next time you're in a closed guard don't just think of getting out, ask yourself how long it took you to do so.

Two mindsets in Jiu jitsu:

When it comes to attacking an opponent there are two mindsets. The first is to decide what form of attack you want to use and impose that upon your opponent. This methodology is all about knowing your own strengths. You know what you're good at - impose those skills upon the opponent regardless of what he is doing and be so good at them that he can't stop you even if he knows your intentions. The second is to observe your opponent's stance and movement and harmonize your choice of attack with whatever opportunity his stance and motion offers. This methodology is all about knowing what attack is appropriate for a given opportunity. The first is a matter of building a small set of highly developed and unstoppable attacks. The second is about building a large set of attacks that only need to be good enough to break through a momentary weakness. Both approaches are highly effective. In my experience the unstoppable attack method is best in shorter matches where there is a discrepancy in skill or size in your favor. The opportunistic attack method does better in longer matches where skill and size are more even - however this is a generalization and there are notable exceptions to this. Over time most athletes gravitate naturally more towards one than the other but most great athletes can play both approaches even though they generally favor one over the other. I generally find the opportunistic method has a smoother and more refined look to it and as I have aged and grown weaker I have favored it more - it generally requires a less physical game. Essentially it is a choice between the ability to amass great strength to smash through very strong defenses vs the ability to see a weakness and quickly attack with adequate strength to break through in the time available. Try to develop both but it's natural that you will probably favor one over the other.

Push and pull:
We don't believe in super powers - you don't have to - the power that good mechanical understanding and efficiency can give you is

more than enough for anything you need to do in Jiu jitsu. The greatest power in Jiu jitsu is the ability to successfully utilize the potential of action and reaction. When you can elicit a push from an opponent and then pull him in the same direction as his push - you will use his own strength to off balance him. LEARNING TO EXPLOIT THE INCREDIBLE POTENTIAL OF ACTION/REACTION IS THE GREATEST STEP YOU CAN MAKE IN JIU JITSU. This is the best means of defeating faster, stronger and more athletic opponents. The key to learning is to engage in push and pull at every opportunity during drilling and sparring and so develop a sensitivity to where your opponent's energy is being directed at any given moment. When you push, feel his push back, and PULL. When you pull him, feel his pull back and PUSH. This sounds simple, but making a habit of it in a hard-sparring match takes time and awareness. What is simple in concept is not so simple in operation. Start small. In drilling out hands on an opponent and start pushing and pulling each other with only moderate force and low speed until you develop an ability to read his energy level and direction and then give a little push when pulled or pull when pushed - try to use the least force you can to get the biggest reaction you can. You can use this EVERYWHERE - standing, ground, top or bottom. It is a foundational principle in most martial arts - make it the foundation of your game and you will add a level of depth and skill that will make you stand out among your peers.

The other side of guard passing:

The single biggest aspect of the Jiu jitsu positional game is the struggle of the top player to get past his opponent's guard (legs) vs the bottom players struggle to get to guard and retain it. It's probably fair to say that that is three quarters of the positional game in Jiu jitsu. When it comes to guard passing, we get taught initially to think mostly in terms of passing guard into side pins. This is good thinking since it accounts for the vast majority of passing outcomes at beginner level. However, as you get higher in the sport and the level of guard play and retention of your opponent's rises, in MANY situations (perhaps even most) you won't be passing to side pins so much as getting defensive reactions from opponents performed expressly to PREVENT you getting to a side pin that expose their BACK to you. The score won't come from passing to side, but rather scrambling to your opponent's back and taking rear mount. In a competitive match the bottom athlete will never willingly concede a side pin and the three points - he will instead turn to his knees - this will always create momentary back exposure. If your mind is only thinking in terms of side pins, you won't react to the new opportunity. WHEN ENGAGED IN A HEATED PASSING BATTLE AGAINST A TOUGH AND SKILLED OPPONENT YOU MUST BE THINKING ABOUT TAKING THE BACK AS MUCH AS THE SIDE. That way when that half second of back exposure occurs you will pounce on the opportunity without hesitation and score. Here Oliver Taza does a good job exposing Gordon Ryan's back during guard drills - the chance won't be there long against an opponent of this caliber - having your mind set in that direction from the beginning lessens the time needed to see an opportunity and pull the trigger!

No one ever said your back has to stay on the ground:
When we first start learning guard position we typically start in supine positions (usually closed guard in most coaching programs). Because we START there we usually tend to STAY there. This can become a problem when an opponent starts passing your guard. As they gain angle and distance and threaten to pass there are many times when it's a good idea to get up off your back to stage some last-ditch resistance and recover. You don't always have to do this - but when an opponent is very close to passing it's often a good idea to get up off your back and post on your elbow or hand to get your shoulders off the mat. This will first, prevent an opponent cleanly pinning your shoulders and head to the mat and completing the pass. Second, give you greater mobility to recover your leg position and put your opponent back in your guard. Like everything in Jiu jitsu (and life) it comes at a price. You can expose your back to a rear mount specialist and your waist to a body lock passing specialist - but sometimes you have to take a risk to prevent a score. If you feel opponents are passing too easily try propping yourself up on hand or elbow to give yourself the mobility you need to recover.

What does it really mean to say you should attack 100% of the human body?
The ideal of Jiu jitsu is to be able to attack specific and vulnerable parts of an opponent's whole body with our whole body. In this regard most, people think in terms of upper body and lower body.

In the last decade Jiu jitsu has made remarkable progress in lower body attacks (a traditional weak area). However, in order to really attack the whole body, you need to go further than just thinking in terms of upper body lower body. For the purposes of submission attacks the human body is best divided three ways

1 - upper body/lower body
2 - left side/right side
3 - front side/back side

In addition, the means of attack - submission holds - can be divided into joint locks and strangles. So, if we are to maximize our attacking versatility - and this should be the goal of all of us if we are to call ourselves submission specialists - then we ought to be able to attack upper body and lower body, left side and right side, from both front and back, with both strangle holds (where appropriate) and joint locks. THAT will allow you to cover all the possible ways in which submissions can be employed against an opponent. You don't need to know a lot of submissions to do this, but you DO need to know how to cover the whole of an opponent's body with them if you are to reliably break through against the toughest opponents. Widen your perspective with this understanding of what it really means to attack the whole body and soon you'll widen your submission arsenal in ways that improve your performance.

When the Gi comes off:
Jiu jitsu is a sport with four faces. Gi grappling, No Gi grappling, MMA Jiu jitsu and self-defense Jiu jitsu. Though they are all part of

the same family there are significant differences between them. When it comes to Gi vs no Gi grappling it's important to ask what the most significant differences are between them and even more importantly - what the consequences of those differences are when you're on the mat trying to improve. The three most obvious differences are simple enough - First, the Gi provides a much greater number and efficiency of strangles. Second, the Gi provides a much greater variety and robustness of grips. Third, the Gi provides much greater friction between the two athletes that slows the pace of the match in most areas. Getting further into the discussion, the idea of GRIP has important practical ramifications. The grips provided by the Gi allow for much greater overall pulling power than the no Gi pulling grips. A grip on the lapel is like a grip on a rope - very robust and difficult to break. None of the basic no Gi grips can compare in robustness to the grips one can make with the jacket and pants, especially when sweat is factored in. The one great exception to this is LOCKED HANDS. Locking your hands around your opponent's waist, head and arm or upper legs (and many other more specific applications) creates by far the strongest and most robust pulling force available no Gi. It is crucial you learn to harness and utilize its power and control. You can't always lock your hands, nor is it always desirable to do so - but when it is - no other no Gi grip gives you such a robust pulling grip that allows you to control the toughest and slipperiest opponents and get to your score or submission.

What's next?

Here is an unpleasant truth. The vast majority of moves you attempt in Jiu jitsu will fail. This is true regardless of your skill level. The better you get, the better the opponents you will face. You both know the major moves of the sport. You both know the most reliable counters. Therefore, the vast majority of the moves you attempt against someone your own size and skill level will fail. Once you realize this, you realize that the most important question is not "what move should I use?" But rather, "what moves will I follow up with after my initial move." Your whole way of thinking in Jiu jitsu must reflect the simple reality that most moves against a well-matched opponent will fail and that you must always think in terms of WHATS NEXT? This is not something you can reliably figure out in the moment - you can get away with that on occasion but it's much better to MAP THE OPTIONS OUT IN ADVANCE. I started with an unpleasant truth. Now let me offer a pleasant one. Against a well match opponent, most moves fail, however, well applied failed moves CREATE VERY PREDICTABLE DEFENSIVE REACTIONS FROM YOUR OPPONENT THAT ARE EASY TO EXPLOIT WITH SECOND, THIRD OR FOURTH MOVES. THAT is where the fight is really won or lost. You know what your best attacks are - now it's time to learn the most common reactions you see to them and map out your responses. In the great majority of cases the match is not won on the first attack, but by the second third or fourth - make sure your training and thinking reflects that.

If you could have a superpower...
Imagine God came to you one night and declared that he wants to give you an entry level super power - not a crazy super power like Thanos or Superman that makes you into a God - but a genuine human level superpower. He gives you a choice. You either choose the ability to make yourself massively stronger than everyone else on the planet, or you can make everyone else on the planet massively weaker than yourself (so you aren't any stronger, but you can make anyone in front of much weaker). Which would you choose? There is definitely a sense in which the first choice is smarter, since if you become much stronger you can apply that new strength to anything - you could use it to fight humans or lift cars or perform tasks that no one else can. The second choice only applies to humans and so would only have value when trying to overcome someone in a match. So, in a fantasy world the first option makes more sense. But what about the real world of Jiu jitsu? Is it smarter for us to focus on greater ourselves stronger? Or making our opponents weaker? Well, I strongly urge you to work on both. As athletes we all have a responsibility to try to improve every aspect of our physicality - it's an important part of performance in Jiu jitsu. However, in the real world there are definite limits on what can be done to improve your strength, speed and stamina. Once you get to a certain level you start to experience diminishing returns on the time invested in training. There is no great difference in sparring against someone who bench presses 400 pounds versus someone who presses 550 pounds in Jiu jitsu. They both feel strong - yet the amount of time and effort it takes to get from 400 to 550 pounds on the bench is very considerable. When it comes to making people weaker however, there are virtually no limits. Small improvements in position, angle, biomechanics, can severely degrade an opponent's strength and overall athleticism and you can keep making improvements forever. We all have a responsibility to make

ourselves as strong as we can - BUT JIU JITSU IS MUCH MORE ABOUT MAKING THE OTHER FELLOW WEAKER THAN IT IS ABOUT MAKING OURSELVES STRONGER.

In a world of many options, focus on the scenarios:
When it comes to selecting techniques, Jiu jitsu offers far more choices than you can realistically master in a life time. Your task isn't to master them all but rather to select a few and spend your Jiu jitsu career mastering those. This begs the question - OK if I'm supposed to learn and master a smaller number of techniques and largely ignore the rest, which ones should I focus on? To a large degree this will be answered organically over time. Your body type and personality will tend to favor certain moves and create an aversion to others. Over time you will invest in those you favor and they will be the bedrock of your game. Your coach will influence your selection also. Every coach has their own philosophy of Jiu jitsu and tends to push that in their teaching and naturally the students tend to think and act upon similar lines to the doctrines they are exposed to daily. You can go beyond this however and start asking yourself what general scenarios always seem to emerge in a given skill area and which need to be covered. For example, in guard passing the basic choice is between standing and kneeling passes. Whichever passes you decide to incorporate into your game, make sure that they cover both standing and kneeling methods. Don't select only kneeling or only standing methods - you need to cover both scenarios. Go further, you need some passes that work through pressure/weight and some that work through

movement/positioning. Make sure you have a solid representative for both approaches. It's good to focus on the moves that come naturally to you, but make damn sure that they cover the main scenarios the sport presents in that domain, otherwise you will be left with an incomplete skill set that a good opponent can take advantage of.

Some moves come naturally and some don't:
I am sure you've all had the experience of learning a move and the first few times you drilled it, it seemed to fall into place very readily. Perhaps later in sparring you got it to work or came close to getting it to work against a tough opponent. It stood out as a move that seemed natural and unforced to you. I'm equally sure you've had the experience of being shown a move that looked valuable but when you drilled it felt very awkward and unnatural. When you tried it in sparring not only did it not work, it wasn't even close and perhaps even got you in trouble. It can't be denied that we all have this kind of experience. The question is, what should we make of it? Should we only focus on the moves that come naturally and ignore the ones that feel immediately difficult? That is certainly tempting and understandable, but we can't take that option. Some moves, for example an elbow escape, are so fundamental and determine so much of our overall potential that they simply cannot be dismissed no matter how awkward and unnatural they might feel when you begin. Some moves are interesting but low percentage, rarely figuring in top level competition. Even if they felt very natural I'd be reluctant to invest huge amounts of training time in that

direction no matter how natural and easy the move felt to me. The right way to think about it is to take the intersection of both considerations. Is it high percentage - that is, is it successfully used by a wide array of athletes across all belt levels, all weight divisions and all body types over a considerable time period? And, does it feel natural in its application for you as an individual, the kind of move you could employ with confidence and power in a very tough high stakes match? If the answer to both is yes - YOU'VE FOUND YOUR MOVE - train it, research it, develop strong follow ups to it and win with it!

The pattern of champions:
In Jiu jitsu and in life, some individuals seem to rise to a level above their peers. It's worth asking if there are any patterns that emerge in this process that perhaps we could emulate in order to improve our own performance in whatever field we wish to progress. There are many factors that I have observed over the years but let's focus on one for today. Jiu jitsu offers an ocean of moves - far more than you could learn in one lifetime. Our lives are short and our minds limited in capacity. So, what are we to do? We are caught in a conundrum. There are ten thousand moves in Jiu jitsu. Any one of those moves could be used by an opponent to defeat us. Yet we can't hope to learn them all in depth as it would take ten lifetimes to do so. The way champions respond to this problem can be stated in a single sentence. To excel in your field - YOU NEED TO LEARN A LITTLE ABOUT A LOT AND A LOT ABOUT A LITTLE. Yes, it's true that there are far more moves than you can ever learn - SO FOCUS ON

A SMALL NUMBER OF MOVES THAT ARE HIGH PERCENTAGE AND FIT WELL WITH YOUR BODY TYPE AND PERSONALITY AND YOUR VISION OF WHAT YOU WANT TO EXPRESS - so learn a LOT about a little number of crucial moves that form your core skill set - they will be responsible for the vast majority of your wins and success. Yes, it's true that any one of the thousands of moves of the sport could be used by an opponent to defeat you - so learn a LITTLE about all of them - just enough so that you have awareness of the danger. As long as you can perceive danger ahead of time you can defend a move with minimal knowledge by disengaging early - ignorance of encroaching danger has gotten more people submitted than all other factors. This is how champions get around THE PROBLEM OF KNOWLEDGE. They learn a lot about a little and seek MASTERY in a small set of skills that make them powerful; and, they learn a little about many moves, just enough to perceive danger early and move away before it's too late. In this world it's impossible to know everything - AND YOU DON'T NEED TO - you just have to know everything about a few things and a little about the rest.

When it all seems confusing...

There are many times when the moves of Jiu jitsu seem damn confusing and difficult to perform even in basic drilling with a cooperative partner - forget about live sparring. Whenever this occurs remember this - every move is a sequence of component moves each requiring mechanical details in order to be effectively applied. For any given move, certain stages in that sequence and certain mechanical details are more important to the overall success and failure than the others. If it ever seems too confusing and complicated - FOCUS ONLY ON ONE OR TWO MAJOR FEATURES OF THE MOVE RATHER THAN THE WHOLE MOVE. If you can adequately perform two components of a six stage move on Monday, then add another on Wednesday, two more on Friday and the last on Sunday - you can perform the move in a week. Don't get discouraged when the whole move doesn't come quickly - focus on the components instead. Your goal is to learn the move - no one ever said you have to learn it all first time around. I would be happier seeing a student learn and competently demonstrate the first stage of an elbow escape in a session than make a hackneyed and clumsy rendition of the whole move that would never work in sparring. In a single workout - BETTER TO LEARN A PART OF A MOVE WELL THAN THE WHOLE MOVE POORLY - you can always learn the next steps next time.

Integration of offense and defense:

Jiu jitsu and fighting in general is always divided into OFFENSIVE and DEFENSIVE skills. This is a useful division when you begin learning as it enables you to focus on a given skill domain. However, as you game matures let's be clear - your ultimate level in the game will not be measured so much by your skills in offense and defense but rather by your ability to INTEGRATE offensive and defensive skills. The final steps of the offense/defense dichotomy is to break down the barrier between them and see that ALL GOOD OFFENSE HAS DEFENSE BUILT INTO IT, AND ALL GOOD DEFENSE HAS

OFFENSE BUILT INTO IT. Your long-term goal is to bring them together to the greatest degree possible at all times.

Know what you want - make a flexible plan to get there:
People who know what they want usually get there. Those who know what they want and have a good plan to navigate their way get there get there often. Those who know what they want and have a flexible plan that adjusts to the many variables and contingencies that life throws at us over time almost always get there. Those that have no idea what they want have to be content with whatever fate gives them - sometimes good, sometimes bad, but never an expression of your will. Your work outs must reflect this pattern. If you come in with no goal and no plan, the worth of your workout will be determined by those around you, sometimes good, sometimes bad, never an expression of a vision you have of yourself as a better player in the future, but only a vague hope that one day maybe you'll be good. If you come in with a clear goal and a plan to enact it that can change intelligently according to changing circumstances over time you will find over time that goals get realized and the you of today beats the you of yesterday, just as the you of tomorrow will defeat the you of today. You carry a lot into every workout - your physicality, tactics, technique, enthusiasm, passion, worries, anxieties, fatigue, injuries, burn out - but the most important thing you can ever bring is A GOAL AND A PLAN.

Next!

The round is over and the next one begins - what's going through your head? Remember always that mental engagement is every bit as important as physical engagement in the sparring rounds. In the time between rounds have a sense of who you want to spar with and what skills you want to work on. If you choose some better than yourself it will be a good opportunity to work on survival and escape skills. If it's someone bigger and stronger it's a good opportunity to work on moving and managing weight from bottom position. If it's someone of lesser skill, then it's a fine to work on control to submission. If it's someone of equal skill, an opportunity to work on wearing an opponent down physically over time to gain tactical advantage over the course of a match. Next time the round ends and you're looking around the room - do so with a plan rather than leaving it to chance.

When you're tired:
All the combat sports are exhausting in their own way. The bad news is - they stay exhausting your whole career. As you get better and better, so do your opponents - so you'll always be under great physical stress that has your body drenched in sweat and chest heaving, utterly exhausted after a rough round. IT'S OK TO BE TIRED - BUT IT'S NOT OK TO SHOW IT. Learning to mask fatigue is an important skill in itself. Your opponent's draw hope and optimism from seeing you exhausted. A tired opponent who is himself thinking of quitting will find renewed energy and drive if he sees you doubled over with exhaustion with the posture of a beaten

man. If you are a competitive athlete (obviously what I am saying does not hold true for recreational athletes, older athletes, beginners or if you're simply out of shape due to interruption in your training routine) When you're tired, practice holding your composure and posture. No matter how hard your heart is beating and lungs burning - stand tall and composed, face neutral - YOUR FACE IS A MASK FOR WHATS REALLY GOING ON INSIDE YOUR HEAD - when an opponent can penetrate the mask he gains strength - when he can't - he loses hope. Controlling your body language under stress is a real skill, and like any skill - it's needs practice - practice begins next time you're feeling like you've got nothing left to give.

Printed in Great Britain
by Amazon